What the Traveller Saw

By the same author

Previous page
The Orient Express. Mighty engine seen from the window of a wagon-lit on the Istanbul Express, 4.25 a.m. Svilengrad, Bulgaria, winter 1964.

What the Traveller Saw

ERIC NEWBY

VIKING
STUDIO
BOOKS

VIKING STUDIO BOOKS
Published by the Penguin Group
Viking Penguin, a division of Penguin Books USA Inc.,
40 West 23rd Street, New York, New York 10010, U.S.A.
Penguin Books Ltd, 27 Wrights Lane,
London W8 5TZ, England
Penguin Books Australia Ltd, Ringwood,
Victoria, Australia
Penguin Books Canada Ltd, 2801 John Street,
Markham, Ontario, Canada L3R 1B4
Penguin Books (N.Z.) Ltd, 182–190 Wairau Road,
Auckland 10, New Zealand

Penguin Books Ltd, Registered Offices:
Harmondsworth, Middlesex, England

First American Edition
Published in 1990 by Viking Penguin, a division of Penguin Books USA Inc.

10 9 8 7 6 5 4 3 2 1   1 3 5 7 9 10 8 6 4 2   1 2 3 4 5 6 7 8 9 10

ISBN 0-670-83123-9
CIP data available

Printed in Great Britain
Set in Itek Meridien
Designed by Ronald Clark

To Wanda – as always

Acknowledgements

I would like to take this opportunity to express my thanks to Ronald Clark of Collins for the truly enormous patience he displayed while designing this book and bringing it to fruition, and to Carol O'Brien and Lucinda McNeile for their equally heroic efforts in the editorial field.

Contents

Introduction

My first camera was a pretty feeble affair. This much was obvious, even to me, when I received it as a present on my seventh birthday. It came from some far-off place I had never heard of up until then. I think it was Lithuania, but there were lots of places I had never heard of at that time. This camera took pictures the size of the smaller sort of Lithuanian postage stamp – that is, when it took any at all – with ludicrous results. It came in a carrying case made of cardboard, together with three rolls of film, and when these were used up the only way to get more was to buy a return ticket to Lithuania.

My next camera was a No. 2 Box Brownie, an Easter present from my parents when I was about ten, bought from a Mr Powell who had a photographic business on the seafront at Swanage, Dorset. I was mad about birds in those days, and it was with a copy of *British Birds and How to Identify Them* (or some such title) and this camera, which had a fixed exposure of approximately 1/25th at *f*/11 (the shutter sounded like a portcullis falling), that I attempted to photograph them. As a result, I had, until recently, a large collection of negatives and prints, 3¼ × 2¼ ins, of the boughs of windswept trees and Purbeck drystone walls from which the birds I was trying to photograph had already flown away. Nevertheless, I loved my No. 2 Box Brownie.

My first precision camera, and one of the best cameras I have ever possessed, was a Zeiss Super Ikonta; a tiny, folding, bellows camera with an F.3.5 Tessar lens, a Compur shutter and a coupled rangefinder which took 16 pictures on 3¼ × 2¼ in roll film. This was the camera I took with me in 1938 on a round-the-world voyage. I didn't have an exposure meter, but by using something known as a Burroughs Wellcome Exposure Calculator, which came in the back of a diary, I got some surprisingly good results, considering how little I knew then, and know now for that matter, about photography. I tried very hard with my sea pictures because I knew that war was imminent, and I had a premonition that it would mean the end of the big sailing ships engaged in the Australian grain trade, and the way of life of the men and boys who sailed them, and I was right. During the war, I took a lot of photographs on the coast of Syria, where life was still very primitive, but when I was captured the authorities in Malta went through my baggage before sending it on to my next-of-kin, and so I never saw these pictures or my Super Ikonta again.

My next chance to take pictures in outlandish places came in 1956 when I travelled through the Hindu Kush. Photographically, the expedition was a disaster. In the course of it an Afghan tribesman who was in charge of the pack horses allowed the one which was carrying all my exposed film to enter a lake and swim across it. As a result, when the film was developed, the negatives looked as if they had been processed in some sort of thin soup.

This is the problem with photography. It is inimical to travellers and to travel. It takes ages to do it properly. You can wait days, months, even years for a crescent moon to appear over the Taj Mahal, and then the camera goes wrong. If a modern one, the nearest place it can be repaired is Hokkaido, Japan. Even there they probably won't repair it. They will simply 'replace the unit', and to do so will take at least six months, for a large part of which it will be stuck in customs. If the camera doesn't go wrong of its own accord, you yourself will inevitably drop it. Now that the exposure meter forms an integral part of the camera (only the most sophisticated photographers have separate meters anymore), you score double by breaking both. Having done this, the only thing to do is to drop the remains in a deep river and tell the insurance company that some-one stole it, otherwise your claim will never be settled. If any of these things happen to you, and you are relying on your camera to take photo-graphs suitable for publication, it can seriously endanger your peace of mind. You therefore need several cameras, just like the professionals. Amateurs almost always have only the one.

After this photographic débâcle in the Hindu Kush, nothing hap-pened photographically until 1962 when Wanda and I descended the Ganges in various sorts of boats. On this journey we both took pictures for the book I was going to write, if we survived, sharing (what folly!) a single Pentax between us, a Weston exposure meter, and using what was then a new colour transparency film called Kodachrome X. Kodak were so pleased with the results – surprised would be more accurate – that they put on an exhibition of our photographs in Kingsway.

One of the further troubles with having a camera is the lengths to which you must go to avoid pictures entirely devoid of human beings. You always have to run on ahead. In the Hindu Kush, it was in order to photograph the caravan approaching, at around 16,000 feet, that I was left at such a height, feeling utterly lifeless. On the Ganges, for the simple purpose of photographing the boat, Wanda and the boatman, I disem-barked, only to find I was in danger of being left alone in the middle of Hindu India as the boat sped away down some rapid. But if you don't run on ahead or go ashore on such journeys, you will end up with pictures of endless mountain ranges and endless reaches of water, and never a person in sight.

Much more important to me than cameras, either on the Hindu Kush or on the Ganges, were my journals; because all that I have ever really needed to record what I needed to record has been a notebook, and one of those Staedtler pencils with a long lead and a sharpener at one end which I always have to be careful not to lose. A pencil is better than a pen because when the paper gets wet the ink runs and the writing becomes illegible. On the Ganges, which was pretty wet, I used as a log book a Gujarati account book with a red linen cover and yellow paper bought in Chandi Chowk, Old Delhi. This I filled with such monumental observations as '9.50 a.m. Left Bank. Saw a tree', and some miles further on, '10.45 a.m. Right Bank. Saw a cow'. From such modest beginnings this book became a tome stuffed with information, some of it curious, a lot of it useless, but something without which I knew that I would never be able to write whichever book I was planning to write. Just as I had kept a log book in the sailing ship without which I could not have written *The Last Grain Race* sixteen years later.

Even the thought of losing the Gujarati account book filled me with apprehension, and then, one day, I did lose it. Waking up in what had been a church hall in Bihar in the middle of the night, plagued by rats, I realized that I had left it on the platform at a railway junction, miles away. Arriving there by cycle rickshaw in what was by then the early hours of the next morning, I found that there had been no cause for alarm. 'Sir,' said the ticket clerk, when he handed it over to me, 'it is only a book of writing, of no value to anyone at all.'

The following year, in 1963, I went to work for the *Observer* as Travel Editor, and a large number of the pictures in this book were taken during that period, one of the happiest periods of my life, which lasted ten years. As a result, *What the Traveller Saw* essentially commemorates the past, and, in many cases, a world that has changed beyond all recognition.

Round the Horn Before the Mast
1938/39

THESE photographs form part of a large collection taken while I was serving in the four-masted Finnish barque *Moshulu* of Mariehamn in 1938/9, when she was engaged in the Australian grain trade.

As an apprentice in *Moshulu* I was bound by the Conditions for the Acceptance of Apprentices in Finnish Sailing Vessels. You had to be not less than sixteen years old and of strong constitution. Two doctors' certificates were required, and one from a clergyman testifying that the applicant was of good moral character. My father had to pay the owner of the ship, Gustav Erikson, a premium of £50 for a year or a round voyage, whichever was the shorter. If I died, he was told, he would get a pro-rata repayment. The apprentice had to supply his own gear and was paid 150 Finmarks a month (about 10s. or 50p), but only at the end of the voyage, and less any deductions (I dropped a hammer overboard in Belfast before we sailed, and the cost was deducted from my pay). An able-bodied seaman got about 650 Finmarks, the sailmaker (because he was exceptionally experienced) about 1400 Finmarks, the steward about 2000, the mates from 1200 to 3000, and the captain about 4000 Finmarks (£20) a month. Not much for such a lonely position of responsibility. He was in his thirties. The oldest member of the crew was the sailmaker, who was nearly sixty.

Being an apprentice, I took nearly all the photographs during my free watch; many of them when I was done-in after long hours on deck, at the wheel, or up in the rigging. If I wanted to record the other watch working in rough weather, it required an effort of will not to fall asleep as soon as I went below, but to turn out again with my camera. Similarly uninviting was the prospect of keeping my daily log of the voyage up to date, which I did for some eight months, without missing a day.

What induced budding sailors to sail in Erikson ships in the 1930s, apart from a few inquisitive English speakers such as myself? The Finns were obliged to because they had to spend three years in square sail before going to navigation school in order to sit for a second mate's ticket in their merchant marine. Numbers of Germans had to do the same in order to get in the time required by their government, until Hitler came to power when they had to serve their time in German ships. A great blow to the Germans was the loss of the Hamburg-Amerika Line's *Admiral Karpfanger*, a four-masted barque sold to them by Erikson, which went missing in the Southern Ocean on her way to the Horn from South Australia with the loss of all 68 hands, including 40 cadets, in 1938 – the same year I joined the *Moshulu*. Norway, Sweden and Denmark had similar arrangements for their sailors, some of whom sailed in Finnish ships.

By the 1930s the grain trade from South Australia to Europe was the last enterprise in which the remaining square-riggers (by 1938 there was still only one ship equipped with an auxiliary engine) could engage with any real hope of profit, and then only

The main mast with all square sail set. The two fore-and-aft staysails are the main topmast and topgallant staysail. In full sail, *Moshulu* was designed to carry 45,000 square feet of canvas.

if the owner exercised the strictest economy and at the same time maintained the utmost efficiency.

The only contender for such a role by the time I joined his fleet was Gustav Erikson from Mariehamn, the capital of the Åland Islands in the Baltic, off the coast of Sweden, the owner of ten ocean-going square-rigged sailing ships. He employed no PROs to improve his image. One of the things that warmed me to him was that he was completely indifferent as to whether anyone liked him or not. It would have been as reasonable to expect anyone to 'like' the Prime Minister or the Inspector of Taxes as to like 'Ploddy Gustav', as he was known. He was only interested in his crews in so far as they were necessary to sail his ships efficiently (the majority who sailed in them had to whether they wanted to or not), and for that reason he ensured that crews were adequately and decently fed by sailing-ship standards (which meant that we were permanently ravenous and dreamt of nothing but food), and that the ships, which were rated 100 A1 at Lloyd's but not insured (only the cargoes were insured), were supplied with enough rope, canvas, paint and other necessary materials to enable them to be thoroughly seaworthy.

He certainly knew about sailing ships. At the age of nine he was

Men aloft bending a mainsail. Twenty-four days out from Belfast we picked up the northeast trade wind in 23°N, 19°W, about 150 miles off the Rio de Oro on the African shore. Here, a fairweather (which means old and fairly rotten) mainsail is being bent to conserve the storm canvas, and the man at the weather yardarm is hauling out the head of the sail, which weighed one and a half tons, and reeving the head earring to a hook on the yard. The yard weighed over five tons.

shipped aboard a vessel engaged in the North Sea trade. At nineteen he got his first command, and from 1902 to 1913, after having spent the six previous years in deep-water sail as a mate, he was master of a number of square-rigged vessels before becoming an owner.

Ships engaged in the grain trade would normally sail from Europe at the end of September or early in October in ballast, pick up the trade winds in the North and South Atlantic and, when south of Tristan da Cunha – more or less half way between South America and Africa – run before the westerlies in 40°S or higher latitudes, according to the time of year, across the southern Indian Ocean. The first landfall of the entire 15,000-nautical-mile voyage might well be the lighthouse on the South Neptune Islands at the entrance to the shark-infested Spencer Gulf in the Great Australian Bight, where the wheat was brought down to the little ports on its shores for loading. A good passage outward bound in ballast was around 80 days – we were 82 days in 1939 but *Pommern* was only 78.

It could be weeks or months before a freight was fixed. No pay was issued by the captain for fear that we might run away. As soon as freight was arranged, the ship would sail to the loading port; but first, miles off-shore, the crew had to get rid of the ballast, shovelling it into baskets in the hold where the temperature was up in the hundreds fahrenheit, hoisting them out and emptying them over the side. It was not possible to jettison all the ballast at once, so one or more trips had to be made to the ballast grounds in the intervals of loading the cargo, which was frequently interrupted by the strong winds that blew in the Gulf. Except in one or two places where there were jetties, the ships had to lie off-shore and load the sacks of grain into their holds from lightering ketches. A 3000-ton barque such as *Moshulu* could carry 59,000 sacks of grain, 4875 tons of it, which was what we loaded in 1939.

Even after waiting sometimes months for a freight, and then loading, which could take another six weeks, Erikson could still make a profit after a round voyage of 30,000 sea miles, 15,000 of them in ballast, even if it took some of his smaller barques 120 days or more to make the homeward voyage. The charterers were not worried; providing it was kept dry, grain was not a perishable cargo, and whoever happened to own it at any particular time on the voyage, for it often changed hands several times in the course of it, was getting free warehousing for his cargo.

The normal time of departure for Europe was between the last week in February and the end of March. A good passage home was 100 days, anything less was very good.

We sailed from Port Victoria, where we had loaded in company with the last great concourse of square-rigged merchant ships ever to come together, on 2 March 1939, bound for Queenstown (now Cobh) in Southern Ireland. *Moshulu* was 30 days to the Horn, well over 6000 miles sailing, and on 24 March, in 50°S, 170°W, she ran 296 miles in 23½ hours with the wind WSW (a day noon to noon in these high latitudes is only about 23½ hours).

She was only 55 days to the Equator from Spencer Gulf, and it seemed possible then that, having accomplished this feat of sailing, she might beat *Parma*'s great 83-day passage from Port Victoria to Falmouth in 1933. In fact she suffered a succession of baffling calms in the North Atlantic and was eventually 91 days

Looking aft from the fore yardarm carrying lower topsails and foresail. Great Southern Ocean, 51°S, 158°W, *en route* for Cape Horn. 26 March 1939, wind WSW, force 11. *Moshulu* never hove to.

Above
A big sea coming aboard and one of the
watch on deck jumps for a lifeline.

Opposite
Wind force 10 – Great Southern Ocean.
Moshulu running 10 knots between great

black walls of water a quarter of a mile
apart, and as high as a three-storey house.

to Queenstown, nevertheless making the fastest passage of the year in
what was to prove to be the last great
Grain Race. The slowest passage that
year was 140 days by *Lawhill*, a very
old Erikson barque.

In 1938 *Moshulu* was the biggest
sailing ship afloat. Built in 1904 at
Port Glasgow for the German nitrate
trade as *Kurt* (she had a twin called
Hans), she was also probably the
strongest. She was 3116 gross tons

and 335 feet long between perpen-
diculars. Her hull, standing rigging,
and most of her masts and yards
were steel. The three square-rigged
masts towered 198 feet above the
keel, higher than Nelson's Column.
Each of these masts crossed six yards,
to which six sails were bent, a total of
eighteen square sails; there were also
seventeen fore-and-aft sails including five headsails. With all this canvas set, which was rare – we never set

royal staysails – *Moshulu* carried
45,000 square feet of sail. The biggest
sails, set on yards which were 95 feet
long, were made from No. 1 canvas
and each weighed more than a ton,
much more when wet.

Moshulu could carry sail when a
lesser ship would have had to heave
to. In 51°S, 158°W on the way to the
Horn, with the wind WSW, force 11,
she was still carrying a foresail.
Three hundred lines were belayed to

pins on the pin rails on deck, or else were led to cleats or bitts. You had to know the name of each one in Swedish – the official language in which orders were given in the Erikson fleet – and be able to find the right one, even on a pitch-black night with seas coming aboard.

Half the foremast hands in *Moshulu* the year I sailed in her were first voyagers – the total complement was 32 – and although many of them were country boys with strong constitutions, all of them, including myself, found the work hard at first. An American wooden clipper of the 1850s, Donald McKay's *Sovereign of the Seas*, 2421 tons, had a crew of 106. The work of handling the great acreage of sail, even with the aid of brace and halliard winches, was very heavy. Thirty-four days out from Port Victoria, two days after we passed

the Falkland Islands on the way home, we started changing sails, bending a complete suit of old, patched fair-weather canvas for the tropics in order to save wear-and-tear on the strong stuff, first unbending the storm canvas and lowering it down to the deck on gantlines before stowing it away below deck. This was always done when entering and leaving the trade winds in the North and South Atlantic, four times in all on a round voyage.

While we were engaged in this work, it started to blow hard from the southeast; then it went to the south, blowing force 9 and then 10 from the south-southwest, when the mizzen lower topsail, a heavy canvas storm sail, blew out. This was followed by a flat calm and torrential rain. In the middle of the following night a *pampero*, a terrible wind that comes

off the east coast of South America, hit the ship when it was almost in full sail, but because the Captain knew his job we only lost one sail.

In these twenty-four hours the port and starboard watches, eight boys in each, took in, re-set, took in and re-set again, twenty-eight sails – a total of 112 operations – bent two new sails and wore the ship on to a new tack twice, an operation which required all hands, including the *kock* (the cook), to perform it.

I was in the port watch. The starboard watch were very unlucky – everyone was unlucky some of the time; they spent eleven consecutive hours on deck, or in the rigging.

Strangely enough, I look back on the time I spent in *Moshulu* with the greatest pleasure, and would not swap it for the highest honours of the land.

Left
North Atlantic. Starboard watch sending a royal sail aloft to be bent to the royal yard, 160 feet overhead.

Opposite
Taking in the fore topgallant staysail. The steel bowsprit was 69 feet long and there was no netting under it, as there was (and still is) in most surviving big sailing ships. This was the most dangerous place to work sail in the entire ship.

Home from Home

Italy, 1942

OF all the countries I have ever been to, Italy is the one I feel and know and understand best, by which I mean that I know Italy intuitively rather than in the sense of having accumulated a mass of factual information about it. Its politics are impossible to understand and its history, apart from its artistic history, peculiarly baffling. One soon gets fed up with Guelphs and Ghibellines. I find that what really interest me most about Italy are its inhabitants.

I was twenty-two years old when I first set eyes on it through the periscope of a submarine. What I saw, against the sun in the late afternoon of an August day in 1942, was a low-lying coast shimmering in the heat, an undulating black line, like some minor tremor on the Richter scale, which might have been anywhere.

That night, when my companions and I hauled our canoes up out of the surf on this same coast, for the first time in my life – although I had travelled something like one and a half times round the world already – I found myself in Europe; that is, if you can actually call Sicily a part of Europe, or even a part of Italy. The important thing is that at that time I thought it was.

My impressions, because of how we had arrived, were somewhat different from those received by more conventional visitors. They were of a sandy shore with surf booming on to it, concrete blockhouses, barbed wire entanglements and, somewhere ahead of us, German dive bombers coming in to land.

After cutting our way through the barbed wire we met our first Italian living thing, an old white horse in a field. It was difficult to think of it as an enemy horse but if it had decided to start whinnying or galloping around it could easily have brought down on us a horde of the enemy. Instead, it preserved a benevolent neutrality and went on eating its dinner.

After this we became imbrangled in a vineyard in which I ate my first bunch of Italian grapes. They were not particularly nice as they were still unripe and had been recently sprayed with what I identified after the war, when I began to learn about grapes and wine, as copper sulphate.

There then followed an encounter with some very nasty dogs in a farmyard – savage dogs on long chains were, I was later to learn, a feature of most Italian farmyards – but after this, as we neared the airfield we had come to attack, we began to have our first encounters with European people, presumably Italians; dark figures who sidled up to us out of a darker darkness, emitting noises that sounded like, 'Eh! Eh! Eh!', and then, getting no reply, disappearing as quickly as they had come, no doubt as frightened of us as we were of them.

How much that, then ostensibly lonely, shore had since changed (in fact it was swarming with German as well as Italian soldiery), was evident when I returned to it a couple of years ago to find a rather low-class seaside resort with *alberghi* and *pensioni* forming a continuous barrier along the shore, which, if they had been there some forty-five years pre-

A side street in Parma, 1963. The man is wearing the now near-extinct cloak known as *il tabarro*, in local dialect *il tabar*.

viously, would have been much more difficult to negotiate than wire entanglements, while the long pipes which now ran seawards from them would have ensured that we were engulfed in sewage even before we set foot on the shore.

The following morning, having spent some hours swimming about in the Mediterranean, and failing to re-join the submarine, with Mount Etna, our first Italian volcano, smoking away overhead, we were picked up by the first Italian fishermen we had ever seen who were sufficiently kindly, having saved our lives, to make unthinkable the idea of banging them on the head and trying to get to Malta in their boat.

And as we chugged into the harbour of Catania I had my first sight of an Italian city beside the sea, as I had always imagined it would be, just as Rex Whistler might have painted it, with baroque domes and Renaissance *palazzi*, all golden in the early morning sun.

We were hurried off the boat and up through narrow streets to a Fascist headquarters with a picture of Il Duce on the wall where, minus our trousers, which we had lost at sea, we met our first Blackshirts. They consigned us to a fortress in the moat of which one of their number, more excited than the rest, said we would be shot at dawn the following day. In spite of not knowing until some time later that this fate had befallen a previous party, we believed him. But we weren't shot. Instead we were taken to Rome and kept prisoners in the barracks of a posh cavalry regiment. Here we tasted our first, real Italian food. It came from the officers' mess and was delicious, *pasta* and *peperoni*, and our first Italian wine. From the window of my room, which was high up under the eaves and very hot, all I could see of Rome was an officer exercising a charger of the tan

in a courtyard. A whole decade was to pass before I would again visit Rome in August.

In the spring of 1943, about nine months after I was captured, a number of us were sent to a rather superior prison camp situated in what is known as the Pianura Padana, the great plain through which the River Po flows on its way from its source in the Cottian Alps on the French frontier to the Adriatic. This camp was in a disused orphanage on the edge of a large village called Fontanellato, which is now very close to the Autostrada del Sole, and the nearest city was Parma on the Via Emilia, the Roman road that runs through the *pianura* in an almost straight line from Milan to the Adriatic.

There, once a week, parties of us were allowed to go for route marches in the surrounding country under a general parole that we would not try to escape, but we were nevertheless still heavily guarded. The route chosen deliberately avoided villages.

We walked along flat, dusty roads on which we rarely saw a motor car, only cyclists and carts drawn by oxen; past wheat fields, fields where what resembled miniature forests of maize (Indian corn) were growing, in which I longed to hide myself and make my escape. We marched along the foot of high, grass-grown embankments, known as *argine*, built to protect the land from the torrents that at certain seasons poured down from the Apennines into the nearby River Po, and also from the Po itself, a powerful, dangerous and unpredictable stream.

We also saw fields of tomato plants that when ripe would be used to make *salsa di pomodoro*, sugar beet, groves of poplars, the trunks of which, soaring up overhead, were like the pillars in a cathedral, endless rows of vines which produced the naturally fizzy red wine known as

Lambrusco. And we saw rambling, red-tiled farmhouses, some of them very large, with farmyards full of cows and pigs and ducks and geese and the inevitable savage dog on a running wire. And there were barns, sometimes with open doors, through which we could see big, mouth-watering Parmesan cheeses ripening in the semidarkness. We were permanently hungry and it was strange to think that, apart from the meals I had been served in the cavalry barracks in Rome, I had never eaten a proper Italian meal in Italy – all the food I had eaten in the prison camps had been cooked by British cooks.

On these walks we saw very few people, probably they were ordered to make themselves scarce. Most of those we did see were *contadini*, bent double working in the fields and all wearing straw hats with huge brims to protect themselves from the fearful heat of the sun. Sometimes they waved but because of these hats it was difficult to know who waved, men or women or both. Others, women and girls mostly, seen momentarily through half-closed green shutters on the upper floors of the farmhouses, also waved a bit apprehensively. No one was obviously unfriendly. And in all these expanses of *pianura* there was not a tractor to be seen.

Our presence in the orphanage provoked lively interest among the inhabitants of our village, Fontanellato, and as the local cemetery was located alongside the orphanage large numbers of them, most of them women, both old and young (the young men were mostly in the armed forces), some of them on bicycles, took more numerous opportunities to pay their respects to the dead than they had done before we arrived on the scene. In fact I first saw the girl I was subsequently to marry on her way to the cemetery

with a group of friends, all of them on bikes. I waved to her from one of the windows overlooking the main road. She waved back and I was shot at by a sentry who was careful to miss, which was a warning against looking out of those particular windows.

On 8 September 1943 the Italian government asked for an armistice. On the following day we all broke out of the orphanage with the connivance of the Italian commandant and took to the countryside to avoid being sent to Germany, which we did by a hair's-breadth.

It was an extraordinary situation. Up to this moment, apart from various interrogators and members of the camp staff with whom we came in contact, few if any of us had ever spoken to an Italian since we had been captured. Now, suddenly, we found ourselves more or less surrounded by the sort of people we had seen working in the fields and riding bikes up the road to the cemetery, most of whom seemed anxious to help us, not, most of them, for any political motive, but because, as they told us, they too had sons and brothers away at the war, many of whom had not been heard of for a long time.

So far as I was concerned the first Italians I now met appeared in the following order: an Italian soldier who led me out of the camp on a mule because I had sprained my ankle and couldn't walk (he then went off with it – 'Vado a casa,' he said, 'I'm going home'); next were a farmer and his wife who hid me in their barn for that first night, who had a son and a daughter; then there was the girl to whom I had waved, by sheer coincidence, who brought me clothes, including one of her father's suits – he was the village schoolmaster; there was a Sicilian doctor, a great friend of the schoolmaster, who arranged for me to be hidden in the maternity ward of the local hospital; then there was its mother superior and various nuns, an elderly male nurse called Giulio who looked and sounded a bit like a walrus, and Maria, a mongoloid child, a permanent member resident in this *ospedale*, who was immensely strong, highly affectionate and used to prove it by going through the motions of strangling me with one of her pigtails, creeping up behind me like a miniature Italian version of an Indian thug.

Until now my fellow prisoners and I had thought of Italians, rather arrogantly, more or less as figures of fun.

We were arrogant because this was one of the few ways in which we could vent our spleen at having been captured, and at the same time keep up our spirits, which were really very low. Before the armistice it is believed that, in spite of innumerable attempts to do so, only two allied prisoners of war actually succeeded in escaping from Italy. This was because Italians of all sorts and conditions were, and are, extraordinarily observant, and all the ingenious subterfuges, disguises and false documents which might have satisfied a German or an English official were hardly ever sufficiently genuine-looking to satisfy even the most myopic Italian ticket collector. It was not only officials. The kind of inspection an allied escaper was subjected to by other travellers in an Italian train compartment would usually be enough to finish him off.

Now, all of a sudden, these same Italians were risking their lives for us, and as I was passed from one helper to the next I began to feel rather like a fragile parcel on its way to some distant delivery point.

It was in this fashion that I arrived at a lonely farmhouse high up in the Apennines, more or less midway between Parma and La Spezia, the Italian naval base on the Ligurian Sea.

There, almost 2500 feet up on what was soon to become, with the onset of winter, the cold, northern face of this 800-mile-long mountain range that forms the backbone of Italy, I found myself suddenly transported, as if by magic, to a way of life that I had never imagined existed in Western Europe, and one that had changed hardly at all for fifty years or more. And there I worked for a farming family who had little enough to eat themselves, in this the third year of the war for Italy, without me to feed, and who lived in the constant, very real, fear of being betrayed by informers for having sheltered me and of being either sent to Germany as forced labourers, or shot.

The people who lived in these remote mountain communities were fighting to survive in an inhospitable terrain. They had always been shorthanded. Even before the war, to make ends meet, many of these mountain men had gone off to work in the industrial areas of northern Italy, France and Switzerland, and even further afield, leaving their wives and children and the aged to fend for themselves as best they could, returning home at rare intervals. Some worked as itinerant knife grinders, others as navvies employed on such superhuman tasks as excavating railway tunnels. Some, more fortunate, had found their way to London where, having found their feet in the catering business, they had been able to send for their wives and families and open little cafés. Some of these men were interned at the beginning of the war and were subsequently drowned when the *Arandora Star*, the ship that was taking them and other internees to Canada, was torpedoed in the Atlantic.

Now many of the young men of these Apennine families were away at the war, many of them with the Giulia division of the Alpini which was now on the Russian front. The only able-bodied men were deserters who had left their units after the armistice, like my friend with the mule at Fontanellato. Like me, they too were on the run, not only from the Germans but also the Fascists, who, after their initial reverse, were making an altogether too rapid recovery.

Up there in the mountains no one except prisoners of war and the deserters, who had to keep an ear open for what was going on, was really interested in the war. For them it was an inexplicable calamity that had deprived many of them of their sons. Few of them were even nominally Fascists, those few that were still practising were, unfortunately, hyperactive.

The villages were collections of grey stone farmhouses huddled together for mutual protection from the elements above a labyrinth of narrow passages which led to the *stalle*, the cowsheds, and barns. These houses were roofed with stone slabs split from the same limestone with which the houses were built.

Apart from the few principal routes, which wound their way up through the Apennines and across the main ridge at one or other of the few passes that could be crossed by motor vehicles, there were few proper roads. Communication between villages was by rough tracks which had probably existed since the beginning of recorded time. Those who used them computed distances by the number of hours it took to reach one's destination, rather than the number of kilometres that had to be covered.

Whenever a road or a track crossed a ridge or reached some other high point there would invariably be a little wayside shrine, usually with the Virgin depicted on a small, Carrara marble slab, of a sort that often dated back to the mid-eighteenth century.

Up there in the mountains, no woman whatever her age thought anything of making a three-hour journey downhill on foot to deliver a consignment of cheese to a weekly market, often carrying it in a first-war Alpini rucksack, and then climbing, loaded with purchases, all the way up again. Pack mules were used to carry heavier loads. Hay and firewood were brought down from the upper meadows and the forests on wooden sledges drawn by cows or bullocks. The only wheeled vehicles were handcarts.

Families lived by growing crops, mostly grain, potatoes and other vegetables, and by milking their cows. They also gathered chestnuts – the flour was a staple food but more so on the warmer, south-facing flanks of the mountains – and also edible mushrooms, such as *boletus edulis*, otherwise *porcini*, a delicacy which commanded high prices and sometimes grew in very large quantities. There were no vines. Vines couldn't exist on this side of the range much above 220 metres, and there were no olives. So olive oil had to be bought. When the snow came in November/December many of the higher farms were often cut off from the outside world for quite long periods, except for those with skis. In this pre-plastic age which endured up here until many years after the war, ploughs were of wood and iron, harrows were made from the trunks of trees, digging was done with a long-handled spade called a *vanga*, nothing like an English spade, which had a triangular blade and a metal projection at right angles to it so that the user could exert more pressure and dig deeper.

Clods were broken up with a two-pronged mattock, called a *zappa*. In a field of any size the work of *zappatura* was hard for a lone operator because up in the mountains the earth was mostly adhesive clay that used to stick on the prongs of the *zappa*. Crops were cut with scythes and sickles.

When working, most of the men wore battered felt hats and what had once been their best Sunday suits. Sometimes they were of corduroy which their wives had repaired so many times, using whatever materials came to hand, that they often resembled patchwork quilts. And under their shirts they wore thick vests, with the natural oil still in the wool, which the women had knitted using wool they had spun themselves.

It was commonplace to see women spinning in the fields while looking after the animals, carrying a wooden spindle tapered at either end and with a perforated stone at the middle of it, to the top of which the woollen yarn was attached, and with the rest of it rolled round a distaff, a piece of wood which they carried tucked under one arm. Until they became old, or widowed, or both, when they dressed in deepest black from head to toe, women and girls for everyday wore dark skirts about the length of a kilt and aprons to protect them when working, blouses, hand-knitted vests, except in hot weather, thick, hand-knitted socks to match, heavy, nailed mountain boots and coloured head scarves. In this society men didn't go to church much. Religion was for women. Among their men it was reserved usually for feast days and for death.

For them, and for me, life in those days when not working outside revolved around the kitchen, the largest, most important room in the house. There was no equivalent to a British front parlour. The fireplace was a blackened cave in which heavy copper cooking pots hung suspended in the chimney by long chains. And there was a cast-iron wood-burning stove with a long silver stove pipe rising from it then executing a right-angled bend before disappearing into one of the walls.

At that time the staple food was homemade bread, baked in an outside oven, using flour which was kept in a piece of furniture known as a *madia*, which had a detachable board on top which was used to make *pasta* – a great standby was a thick vegetable soup made with beans and *pasta* – and there was *polenta*, made with chestnut flour or maize. There was cheese and very rough wine, and for breakfast bread and milk and acorn coffee. Sugar was a black-market commodity; worst of all was the shortage of salt.

After the evening meal they all enjoyed sitting round the fire telling and listening to stories. At that time there were still storytellers whose stories dated back to medieval times, when the Saracens infested the coasts of Italy, stories which had been passed down by word of mouth.

Parma in the winter of 1944, when I was recaptured, was a city of the dead, like the rest of Italy, gelid, without heat, or hope, the Allies bogged down hundreds of miles to the south. It was also a city of terror, under the SS, the Wehrmacht, and the last of the Fascists, all of whom I had seen fleetingly on the way to be imprisoned in the Cittadella, the huge, star-shaped fortress on what were then the outskirts of the city, and when the gates finally closed on me I knew that, for the foreseeable future at least, it was the end of my newfound friendship with Italy.

Below
Parma. Well-to-do farmers meeting in Piazza Garibaldi in the 1960s. Most of them would have voted communist, and probably still do. I remember them standing there during the war in 1944 when I was a prisoner on my way to Germany. Immobilized

by the cold, they looked like strange birds, wearing their *tabarri* with the long end thrown over one shoulder rather like a Scottish plaid. It was a city of terror then under the SS, the Wehrmacht, and the *Repubblichini*, the last and nastiest of the Fascists.

Overleaf
Farmers near Fosdinovo, northern Tuscany. The one on the right is known as 'Pilota' because, in the Second World War, as a member of the Alpini, he was brought back from the Russian front in an aeroplane.

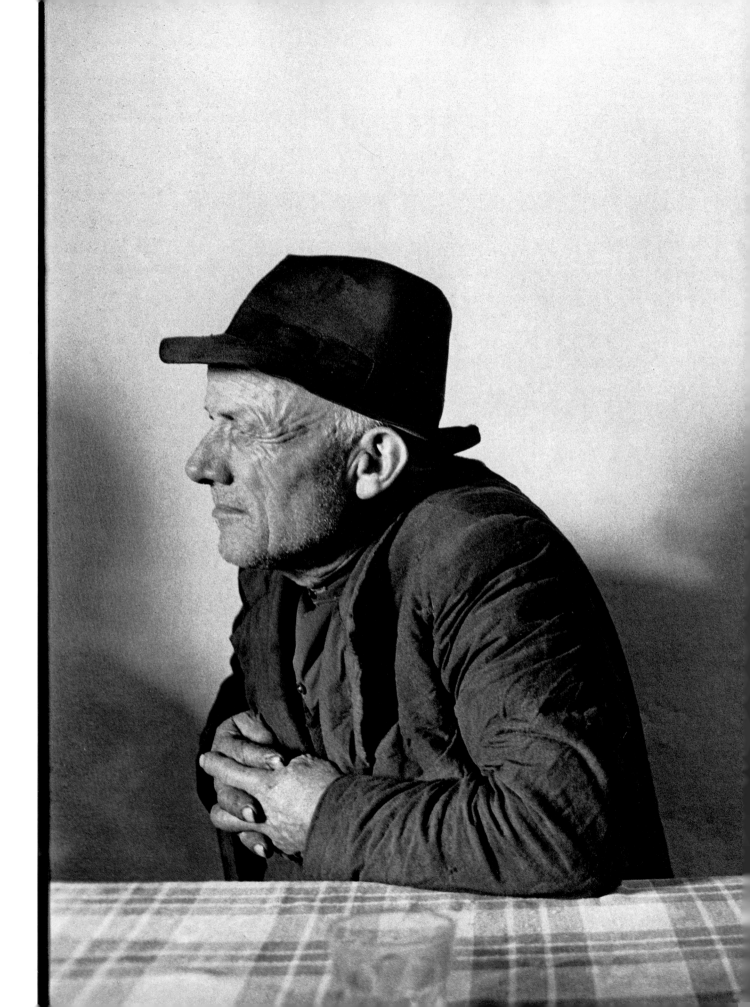

Left and Opposite
The Festa of San Remigio in the town of Fosdinovo. Where we live, the harvesting of the grapes rarely, if ever, takes place before the Festa of San Remigio, which is on 1 October. It was San Remigio who baptized Clovis, King of the Franks, and whose stone effigy stands high above the altar in one of the town's two churches. When we first attended the festa in 1960 almost all the artefacts were the product of a pre-plastic age, made by hand to last a lifetime: harness, ploughshares, copper cauldrons, wheels, pack saddles for mules, broad-ribbed corduroy that wore like iron, nailed boots, wooden mousetraps, thick, hand-knitted socks and vests. And there was (and still is) plenty to eat – big, crusty sandwiches filled with roasted pig – and, until recently, there were open-air drinking booths under the plane trees where you could sit and munch your *panino* and drink the previous year's wine at tables with white cloths on them.

The *vendemmia* – grape harvest – near Fosdinovo.

Below
A farming family, the Dadas, at Sunday lunch near Fosdinovo, northern Tuscany, in 1973. By this time the widespread withdrawal from the land had already made itself felt. For the first time farmers' sons and daughters were being educated and links that had forged them to the land since time immemorial were being broken. Some of these children, the children of our neighbours, came to stay with us in England and later we attended their weddings, and after that various christenings.

Below
A *gondoliere* awaits a suitable customer on the Riva degli Schiavoni outside the Albergo Daniele in Venice.

Opposite
The Riva degli Schiavoni with, in the background, San Giorgio Maggiore.

Whenever I come back to this utterly enslaving, beautiful, stinking, dying city, I do so with the hope that this time it will yield up its secrets to me. But when the time comes for me to leave, I realize that even if I wanted to stay in Venice for the rest of my life this could never be.

In *Albertine Disparue* Proust writes of entering a network of *calli*, the little alleyways of the city, and coming by chance upon a great open *campo* in the moonlight and failing to find it again the next morning, wondering whether it was part of a dream or a place like one of those oriental palaces 'to which mysterious agents convey by night a person who, taken home again before daybreak, can never again find his way back to the magic dwelling which he ends by supposing that he visited only in a dream'.

Early morning, Piazza San Marco. Thinking
about starting work on the façade of
Vincenzo Scamozzi's Procuratie Nuove on its
southern, Caffè Florian, side.

An Officer of the Guard on his way to the
Palazzo del Quirinale, official residence of
the presidents of the Italian Republic, who
mostly take jolly good care not to live there.
It stands on what is one of the seven hills of
Rome.

Above
A village in Molise.

Opposite
A hearse on the premises of Bellomuno
Undertakers (*Impresari di pompe funebri*) on
the Rampo del Campo in Napoli which is
strategically sited on the way to the principal
Neapolitan cemeteries.

Across the Oxus

Kabul–Moscow–Vienna, 1956

T HE cheapest way to get back to Western Europe from Afghanistan in 1956, as I discovered after my unsuccessful attempt to conquer the Hindu Kush, was to fly Aeroflot. I therefore paid a visit to their Kabul offices, which at that time were located in a large, non-committal-looking private house fitted with several doors, none of which opened when I either rang bells or banged on them. After a long interval in which I could distinguish the voices of a man and a woman in what sounded like intimate conversation somewhere inside the building, one of the doors did open and I was led into the office of the manager, a Mr Scholkonogov, an assertive monoglot Russian in a bright blue suit, for whom one of his aides, a crop-haired gentleman, all smiles, interpreted.

I told Mr Scholkonogov that I wanted to fly to Venice.

'Why?' he asked.

It seemed a strange question for the manager of an airline to ask a potential passenger, but at this time I was unused to Russians.

'Because my wife and children are in Venice,' I said. It was no good complicating matters by telling him that they were, in fact, in a village between Trieste and Monfalcone.

'Better you fly to Tirana,' he said, with the air of someone who had already made up his mind that that was where I was going whether I wanted to or not.

'But Tirana's in Albania, it's miles from Venice,' I said. With a man like this unless I watched my step I would probably end up in Siberia.

Happily this was not his intention. He was a nice man, trying to look after my interests. 'Better you go to Tirana because Tirana is much cheaper fare; but if Tirana no good, go to Vienna. Vienna for you still very cheap.'

'How cheap?'

'Very cheap. You buy Afghanis [the Afghan currency] on the black market with English pounds at 150 Afghanis to the pound. Then you buy a ticket from me in roubles at a very good rate of exchange' – I forget what it was – 'and the entire journey Kabul–Vienna by Moscow will cost you . . .' – at this point there was a halt in the conversation during which he got out an abacus and went to work on it, eventually coming up with a figure – '8650 Afghanis, £51. Good for 6000 kilometres. Why not go to England?' – more work on the abacus – 'That will cost you only 10,000 Afghanis, £8 more, and we will both come with you. We have always wished to see England.'

'I can't do that, I've got a wife and children waiting for me in Venice.'

'Mr Scholkonogov asks me to tell you that wives and children are nothing but trouble,' the interpreter said as I prepared to set off for the Bazaar right away, apprehensive that the black market in sterling might suddenly collapse. 'He will telephone our Embassy and tell Mr Oleynik there that it is all right as far as we are concerned for a visa to be issued for you. You should have no difficulty, but go there at once before what Mr Scholkonogov says to Mr Oleynik is forgotten.'

The plane was an Ilyushin 12, a

Russian version of a Dakota. The windows were fitted with lace curtains and the headrests with antimacassars, the only concessions to luxury in this otherwise austere machine. The effect was curious. All that was lacking was an aspidistra. It remained less than half full all the way to Moscow, in spite of people getting on and off, which would scarcely be the case today.

The stewardesses were monolithic. They gave us sweets with the air of schoolmistresses providing the most disagreeable of their pupils with some undreamed-of treat, but no sooner had we put them in our mouths and begun sucking them than we were told to put on our oxygen masks – there was no such thing as one of those mindless, preliminary demonstrations which all too often send the recipients of this vital information to sleep – so we had either to swallow them or spit them out.

Now we were off, on the crossing of the Hindu Kush. Sadly I looked down on snow-covered summits that I now knew, in my heart of hearts, I would never conquer. And then we had to put on our masks in earnest.

With the mountains behind us we were over the Oxus, seeing dense jungle, momentarily, and coming in to land at Termez, on its right bank, in Russian Uzbekistan, where we were out of sight of the river, which I longed to see, a magic one to all explorers.

From Termez we flew northwards to Tashkent, over the Zeravshan and Turkestan Ranges, and over Samarkand, all of which I identified using the Oxford University Economic Atlas of the USSR, which I had bought in the Bazaar at Kabul.

There, in a fearfully gloomy small hotel – who was I to complain where bed and board was part of the £51

ticket? – we dined interminably in the restaurant of the hotel. It took more than an hour for the first course to arrive from the time we sat down at our various tables. The other guests were mostly emancipated male Uzbeks – no Uzbek women were present – all of whom were dressed in Western clothes, although some of them still wore their characteristic, embroidered skull caps. They were more at ease in their suits than they were with the Western cutlery with which they had been provided. More happy, as I would have been, given gristly lumps of mutton to deal with, to have picked them up and tackled them by hand, instead they stuck their forks vertically into them with one hand, while they sawed away with their knives at an angle of forty-five degrees to the meat with the other, so that the effect of numbers of them doing this at once was like the string section of a large orchestra playing away out of tune, on miniature versions of the double bass or cello.

What was by now only relatively modern Tashkent had been built soon after the Trans-Caspian railway reached what was then the Tashkent Oasis in 1898. It was already in the process of being knocked down and replaced by even more gimcrack structures. Later it was to be flattened by an earthquake. Most of the old Uzbek houses in the parts I was able to visit had either been razed to the ground or were in the process of being demolished. Any Uzbeks who retained anything of their native garb, apart from the skull cap, were very old indeed. Walking about the city in this fashion, gazing more or less open-mouthed at everything, I was very soon taken into custody by two plain-clothed policemen, who demanded from me the piece of paper giving the name of my hotel and my room number and on receiving it speedily returned me to it.

Early the following morning we flew northwestwards, following the line of the Syr Darya river and the railway from Tashkent to Moscow, a line on which I had always longed to travel. To the east the milk-chocolate-coloured expanses of the Betpak-Dala Steppe, stamping ground of nomad hordes, stretched away in the direction of Lake Balkhash, four hundred miles or so to the east, while immediately below the river wriggled through what appeared to be desert like an endless, greyish green snake.

Then we landed at Dzhusaly, about a hundred miles east of the Aral Sea, on a military airfield out of sight of the river, out of sight of everything except an endless noth-ingness of steppe. A searing wind was blowing and the air was filled with the high-pitched screamings of Soviet jet fighters warming up for a practice sweep over those parts of Kazakhstan which today are some of the most secret and difficult-to-get-at areas of the USSR. Then we took off again, seeing the Aral Sea shimmer-ing in the sun, on a short trip to Aralsk at its northern end, where we took on more fuel, after which we crossed the southern outliers of the Urals and were in Europe. At Uralsk we ran into a big electric storm and there the pilot altered course to fly north of what was the normal route, which would have taken us straight across the Volga to Penza, but still flying parallel to it. From now on, we flew very low over endless forest.

Twenty-five minutes after passing over Uralsk, on our new course, I looked down on what, if it was not the first missile site I had ever seen, was a very complex sewage farm, a series of dome-shaped concrete con-structions, sprouting up in what looked like newly-made clearings in the forest, like freshly-emergent mushrooms, with what looked like railway lines running out from them.

It was only for an instant; then they were out of sight and the forest closed in again, with occasionally a ride or firebreak running through it to interrupt its endless monotony. Thirty minutes later we crossed the Volga and I asked the least taciturn of the two standing stones which acted as stewardesses to ask the pilot, who up to now had not exactly been a mine of information so far as his passengers were concerned, at what speed we were travelling, informa-tion which he rather surprisingly provided. It was now possible to work out, longitudinally, the approximate position of my missile site/sewage farm, whatever it was. The military attaché at Kabul should be proud of his pupil, I thought. After all, it was he who when I was about to depart had gruffly told me to 'keep my eyes skinned' in case I saw any-thing interesting, and had provided me with a telephone number in Lon-don to ring if I did.

At Moscow I was put up at the Embassy and was invited by the Ambassador (Sir William Hayter) to travel with him the following day to the monastery at Zagorsk to which he was taking Isaiah Berlin who was also staying on the premises. Fool-ishly, perhaps, I turned down this invitation. I wanted to see Moscow and the Muscovites. An Orthodox monastery, however splendid, I felt, could wait. In the event it awaited me for more than twenty years, until 1977.

The Embassy at this time had a particularly beleaguered air about it and the Ambassador said that until recently the only place where he could be reasonably sure of having a conversation without being over-heard by the Russians was in the Embassy garden; but even this was

Below
Church and State. Monks and the Civil Administrator of the Troitsko-Sergievska Lavra, the Trinity Monastery of St Sergius, at Zagorsk.

For almost 550 years Zagorsk was called Sergiev, after the saint who lived and died there. In 1930 it had the honour of being renamed Zagorsk, after Vladimir Zagorski, Secretary of the Communist Party, who was blown up by a bomb in Moscow in 1919.

When we asked this trio whether membership of the Church in the USSR was declining or increasing, and what was the estimated number of members, we received the reply, 'We don't know,' after which we gave up and concentrated on the monastery.

Opposite
Red Square, Moscow. Early morning brush-up.

now no good with the recent improvement in listening devices. Now the only really satisfactory thing to do was to wait until winter if one had something confidential to communicate when it could be done while skating with one's confidant on some frozen lake – summer was no good, boats could too easily be bugged. What about bugged skates? I wondered.

At Sacher's Hotel in Vienna, where I had booked a room while still in Kabul, in spite of my outlandish appearance I was given a splendid double room with a sunken bath, approached by steps, that looked as if it might have been used by Rudolph when it was too damp to make love at Mayerling, and from it I sent Wanda a telegram. 'Hotel Wonderful, come at once,' I said, not realizing that she had not received my first cable from Moscow telling her which wonderful hotel she was to come to. After telephoning the tourist office in Vienna (whose staff might have displayed a little more initiative than they did by telephoning round one or two of the more wonderful Viennese hotels on her behalf) to ask the whereabouts of the Hotel Wonderful, she gave up and waited for me to appear at Trieste.

At this time (the autumn of 1956) Vienna had only recently ceased to be an occupied city, the Treaty restoring Austrian independence having only been signed in May the previous year, and its walls were still covered with allied military graffiti. Otherwise there was little outward sign, except for a certain threadbareness, that it had been occupied for ten years.

The Habsburgs still dominated the city. What they had made and what they stood for was everywhere, above and below ground, embalmed and in the spirit. In the Imperial Vaults, the Kaisergruft, there were

138 of them sealed up in giant catafalques and sarcophagi, one of which weighed eight tons, row upon row of them, as if in some funereal bedding department; dead from suicide, murder, assassination, the firing squad and natural causes, presided over by Franz Josef II, the penultimate Habsburg, who died in bed. The hearts of sixty-four of them were in the Augustiner-kirche. Their intestines, which in life they cosseted at the sulphur springs at Baden, were in St Stephen's. Their dull, nineteenth-century furniture was in enfilades of rooms in the Hofburg. Their jewels and regalia and those of the Holy Roman Empire in its Secular Treasury: the Imperial Crown made for the coronation of Otto the Great in 962, the Orb, the Holy Lance and the Inalienable Heirlooms, the Agate Bowl and the Unicorn, representing the mystical element in medieval kingship which the splendid objects in the Ecclesiastical Treasury next door were somehow less successful in doing. And their uniforms could be picked up for a song, ankle-length coats and sledges to go with them, in the Dorotheum, a huge, rambling pawnbroker's and auction rooms in the Dorotheergasse while sour-faced descendants of their female domestic servants, all dressed in black, dispensed delicious pastries at Demel, an extraordinary Kaffee-Konditorei near the Hofburg in the Kohlmarkt.

Everywhere I went I was confronted by noble, baroque Habsburg façades behind which the present inhabitants, many of them professional people, lived in conditions of gross overcrowding, lacking almost every amenity, although those Viennese in what had been the Russian sector were far worse off. Without industry, without an empire, out on a limb on the furthest frontiers of the West, the city gave the impression that it was dying. Even the young, who spoke of London as if it were Sodom, rather enviously I thought, seemed strangely old when I met them in the wine cellars, which were fun but rather conventional.

After a couple of days of this, replete with Habsburgs and Sachertorte, fed up with the bossy waitresses at Demel and with the very gemütlich chambermaid who every morning used to ask me why I was still 'allein' in such a large, fine, double-bedded room, and awash with coffee over which I sat interminably in a café – the Hawelka, in Dorotheergasse, hung with paintings by Cocteau, Chirico, Dali and Rops – I gave up what was to have been the holiday of a lifetime and took the train to Trieste.

Back in London I was invited to present myself at an office of the Secret Service off Whitehall, staffed by men some of whom I had regarded as being distinctly unstable when I had known them during the war. They were quite thrilled with my sewage farm and I spent a couple of days 'helping them with their enquiries'. On both days I was taken to a dreary pub on the corner of Trafalgar Square, where I was forced to pay for my own sandwiches as apparently they had no appropriation for expenses of this kind. In future, I decided, they could jolly well find their own Russian sewage farms, and I have never again engaged in any remotely clandestine activity for Britain, or for any other country.

Imperial Garden, Vienna. An appropriate end to a 3200-mile flight with Aeroflot, meals and accommodation included, for £51.

Returning from Mass, Inisheer.

When I first went to Aran, back in 1966, the islanders still wore their own distinctive costume, but to a greater extent on Inisheer and Inishmaan. The men wore thick trousers of homespun tweed, which were split up the side seams so that they could be rolled up when launching their boats, and these were kept up by belts with tassels on them, called *criosanna*; thick flannel shirts dyed indigo; and waistcoats made from a hairy, grey-blue tweed. They all wore caps.

The older women still wore very full red flannel skirts and petticoats, which they dyed a shade of madder. All of them wore shawls; some of them already valuable heirlooms. The brown Galway shawl was already extremely rare. Until recently, all the wool for the flannel and tweed used by the islanders had been woven in Galway, but the mill had been burnt down, and although I did manage to find them an alternative source of supply, at least for the indigo flannel, I don't think they ever made use of it. A sort of fatalism had set in.

The Edge of the Western World
Ireland, 1960

'YOU must ask the Captain but he's not here,' the old man said when we asked him if we could visit the house, but not brusquely as he would have done in England, and with no suggestion that he ought to be given something for being rooted out of his habitation late on a winter's afternoon. He had emerged from a Gothick lodge so narrow that one wondered if he had to go to sleep standing up in it.

He unpadlocked and opened an iron gate, which sounded as if it had not been moved on its hinges since the discovery of oil, and admitted us to the 'demesne'. Dusk was coming on. A long, seemingly endless ride between huge, shattered trees eventually led to a rather severe, late-eighteenth-century mansion with its façade intact, but which proved when we reached it to be nothing more than a shell. It had either been burnt, if so probably during the Troubles in the 1920s, or someone had taken the roof off to avoid paying taxes. It was at the time of the Troubles, we found out from the old man later, but alone with it in the gloaming there was no way of knowing. The Captain was away, somewhere across the water. And when in residence he lived in a bungalow.

Over the house rooks circled ceaselessly, below there was a lake full of reeds. To one side there was an artificial mound overgrown with impenetrable thorn, and an obelisk choked with ivy rose from it, like a huge tree trunk.

The whole place had an air of indescribable melancholy about it,

but exercised an irresistible fascination for people such as myself, lovers of the abandoned and the decayed. In Ireland local authorities and developers have a habit of dynamiting these kinds of remains. But there still are hundreds, and perhaps, in spite of such uncontrolled demolitions, thousands of similar places; many of them with lodges from which old men emerge to unlock gates; and sometimes with invisible captains, Foulenoughs and Grimeses some of them, in the offing, for this was a country, as Waugh's Captain Grimes said, where you couldn't get into the soup however hard you tried.

It was the thought of all the people, many of them still alive, who had lived in Ireland but no longer did so, that gave the country its unique feeling of loneliness. Roads led from no place that was or could be signposted, to another, equally nameless, because there was nothing there to signpost. Here, out in the boondocks, women, many of them old, and children, walked long distances; the children to school, the women to weekly markets, there and back. Wherever we went we travelled with a Land Rover full of them, and heard some fine talk of a sort that had simply ceased to exist in modern Britain.

But in spite of this the past was too much for Ireland and its maddening, enchanting people, and sometimes for us, too. In it the ghosts of its past occupants cried out or whispered from empty castles, abandoned islands, hidden loughs, huge, precipitous cliffs (Croaghaun on Achill

Island looms 2192 feet above the sea), burial mounds, caverns, towers, abbeys, churches, follies, waterfalls, holy wells, pasturing places, deserted villages; and from nineteenth-century barracks, middens on the edge of enormous sand beaches, from mountain tops and offshore rocks on which innumerable saints once lived in solitary contemplation.

Opposite
Girl on Achill Island, County Mayo.

Achill Island has the highest sea cliffs in the British Isles, falling 1950 feet to the sea, at an angle of about sixty degrees. From the highest point, a great walk is downhill by the cliffs northwards to Saddle Head (512 feet above the sea, four miles of huge precipices, in places over 900 feet high). Eastwards are the remains of Slievemore village on the southern flanks of a mountain of the same name, a great quartzite cone, 2204 feet high, shot with mica. The village was abandoned in the late nineteenth century, but

continued to be a *buaile* (a milking or pasturing place) to which the islanders resorted in the summer months, living in the 'booley houses'. To stand at dusk in the single street, which is nearly a mile long, with its roofless stone houses and huts on either side, is a moving experience.

Above
A field on Inisheer.

All three of the Aran Islands are little more than bare sheets of limestone from which the labour of succeeding generations has removed by hand what must be millions of stones. They piled these up to form a labyrinth of drystone walls, which also acted as windbreaks. In the countless thousands of

small enclosures so formed, the soil had also been manmade, by the laying down of alternate levels of sand and seaweed. The principal crop was potatoes (a boiled Aran potato was one of the most delicious culinary treats in the world), and cabbages and carrots were also grown. The grass is excellent, and when the cattle have been fattened they are made

to swim out to the ship from Inisheer and Inishmaan to be taken to market in Galway, sometimes drowning *en route*. The last time I visited the islands, in 1986, the deck of the steamer to the islands was full of potatoes in plastic sacks which had come from Holland.

Below
Curragh and crew (with dog) on Inisheer, one of the Aran Islands, County Galway.

Bottom
This Inisheer man is wearing the traditional tweed waistcoat, the approved style of hat, and may well be wearing the flannel shirt under his Aran sweater – a very different object from the rather pansy cream ones with blobs on which are sold as 'Aran knitwear'.

Below
Curragh at sea. Inisheer women in their best going-ashore clothes being rowed out to the steamer that will take them to Galway.

For fishing and transporting passengers and goods to and from the visiting steamer (except on Inishmore Island, the largest and most up-to-date, where the ship can tie up alongside), the islanders, as do many other

communities on the west coast, use *curraghs*. These rowing boats are about nineteen feet long, and have square counters and bows with a pronounced turn-up to help them through the surf. They consist of a light framework of laths covered with tarred canvas. The oars are tapered laths, almost bladeless, which fit over a single thole pin, enabling them to be left unshipped in the water while the crew is fishing. They are very handy but take a bit of getting used to, being what might be described as tender. They can carry phenomenal quantities of people and goods – up to twelve people (the usual crew is three) – and over a ton of potatoes if the weather is good. Sometimes they even carry tomb stones. When not in use, the *curraghs* are left upside down on the shore above high water and look like shiny black monsters. Going to sea, the crews carry them down to the water upside down on their heads, a sight which could be mistaken for some strange, multi-legged creature dreamed up by Hieronymous Bosch. Nowadays, many *curraghs* are equipped with outboard motors.

Below

The Holy Well near the Doon Rock, Kilmacrenan, County Donegal. The stone used for the inauguration rituals of the O'Donnells, Lords of Tyrconnell, is at the south end of this rock. Giraldus Cambrensis, the medieval Welsh topographer, gives a disagreeable, probably imaginary, account of the ceremony in the latter part of the twelfth century: the chief performed his ablutions in soup made from a freshly slaughtered white cow, and his tribesmen subsequently drank it.

The well is at the foot of the hill on which the rock stands. Nearby, in the green grass, there was an extraordinary bed of relics. Dozens of sticks stuck in the ground were wrapped in rags, pieces of lace, silk and cotton, together with handkerchiefs, scarves and unidentifiable articles of clothing – some of them brightly coloured – rosaries, beads and pins. Facing them, one had the impression of being in the presence of a tribe of ragged midgets. A similar place, but much more beautiful, is a well near St Berrahert's Kyle, a church he founded on the south side of Glen Aherlow, in County Tipperary, in the seventh century. But there are many such places in Ireland.

Right

Daigh Bhride (Brigid's Vat), Liscannor, County Clare.

On the side of the hill, which eventually falls away in the huge precipices of the Cliffs of Moher, the waters of a Catholic holy well emerge from the rock in a little whitewashed building constructed by Cornelius O'Brien, an eccentric MP, who was not even a Catholic. This is reached by a narrow, curving passage filled with images and *ex voto* offerings which included crutches thrown away by those miraculously cured. If you see an eel while taking the water, your wish will be granted. Outside, on a little mound filled with flowers in spring, and especially beautiful when the fuchsia are in bloom, are images of the saint in what look rather like telephone boxes. It is a magic place.

Overleaf
Nearby there is a little inn where, until fairly
recently, you could borrow a violin from the
proprietress – three violins hung on hooks
behind the bar – and play, but now the place
has been smartened up.

Butchers are called victuallers in Ireland, and the butchers have the peculiar but rather pleasing foible – at least, to non-vegetarians – of using their knives to scour designs on the sides of their meat. Some of these designs are strikingly similar to those once produced by Maori tattooists in New Zealand.

Below
Strange occupants of a house in
Ennistymon, County Clare.

Overleaf

Are Irish pubs on the way out? In 1985 they were down to eleven thousand in southern Ireland; by 1986 a thousand more had disappeared. Sixteen years ago Ennistymon in County Clare, a place which had 1013 inhabitants, not all of them old enough to have a drink, had 48 pubs. At the last count, which I made with the aid of a local publican in 1986, there were 21 pubs, and other closures were imminent. In fact, it was difficult to tell simply by looking at some of them whether they were closed for the day or for ever. But all is not lost. Cahirciveen, in County Kerry, with about 1550 inhabitants, but shrinking, still had between fifty and sixty pubs, although one reckless fellow put the number at 62.

Mother Ganges

India, 1963

At two o'clock in the afternoon of 6 December 1963, my forty-fourth birthday, Wanda and I set off to travel down the Ganges by boat from Hardwar, one of the most venerated Hindu bathing places, which lies at the feet of the Siwalik Hills. Our destination was the Bay of Bengal, 1200 miles away. The vessel was a five-oared rowing boat and it looked very much like an oversize Thames skiff – it had probably been built by some British official in a moment of nostalgia for the Thames at Henley. Now it was the property of the Executive Engineer of the Irrigation Works on the Ganges Canal, who was an Indian. He had only lent it to us, and then with extreme reluctance, because we had shown him a letter, signed by Mr Nehru, ordering all and sundry to help us on our way down the river.

The boat was twenty-five feet long, had a five-foot beam, was made of mild steel put together with rivets and needed thirty-two people to carry it. This was the number of barefooted men I had paid to carry it across a mile of almost red-hot shingle to the Ganges from the Ganges Canal.

With us was a rather too-high-caste companion for such a journey, procured for us by the personal intervention of Indira Gandhi, acting on behalf of her father, who warned us that he wouldn't stay the course – he didn't – and, for this first part of the journey, three boatmen.

Among the things we had with us was a canvas bag full of books, a Janata oil stove, hurricane lamps, 8 kilos of rice, a small sack of chilli powder, flour, vegetables, a teapot, a kettle, a number of *lathis* (weighted bamboo poles) for hitting dacoits – robbers – on the nut, and military maps with which we had been supplied by the Director General of Ordnance of the Indian Army, who had also obligingly allowed us to acquire some bottles of Indian Army rum.

Two hundred yards below the bridge at Chandi Ghat from which we set off, the boat went aground on great, slimy stones the size and shape of cannon balls, which we had to lift to make a passage for it. Difficult to describe the emotions we felt aground on a 1200-mile boat journey within sight of our point of departure.

What makes the Ganges a great river, and in this sense the greatest of all rivers, is that for more than 450 million Hindus, and for countless others dispersed throughout the world, it is the most holy and most venerated river on earth. To each one of them it is *Ganga Mai*, Mother Ganges. For a Hindu to bathe in her is to be purified of all sin. To say, with love, the words '*O, Ganga! O Ganga!*', even when far from her banks, can atone for the misdeeds of three previous incarnations. To be cremated on them, preferably having died there, and have one's calcined bones scattered on her bosom, or to cast those of one's deceased parents on it, is the ardent desire of every Hindu.

Even before death, sick and aged people who have the means to do so, and others who have not, make what are often long journeys to spend their last days by her side. Some reside in little huts, while those *in extremis* endeavour to have themselves immersed in her so that their sins may be washed away while there is still life in their bodies.

And to drink the water, having bathed in it, and to carry it away in vessels for future consumption – both confer great merit. Many devout Hindus drink no other water, and those who live at a distance contrive to receive regular supplies of it, for Ganges water has extraordinary qualities. Bottled at one of the sacred bathing places, or anywhere else for that matter, it will keep for at least a year. Taken aboard outward-bound ships in the days of sail on the Hooghly near Calcutta, it is said to have outlasted all other waters. It also seems to have a genuine capacity for absorbing germs and rendering them innocuous. We drank it unboiled in the fifty-mile stretch of the river after it first enters the Indian Plain, and boiled and made into tea thereafter for most of the rest of its course without any unfortunate effects. Yet whenever we left the river for one reason or another, we invariably became ill. I would not attempt to explain this. I only state it as a fact.

What confers on the Ganges this unique holiness among rivers? It was not always so. The first Aryan invaders of India thought more highly of the Indus. It was much later that they gave Ganga the highest position and called her Sursarit, River of the Gods. The Ganga emerges under the name of Bhagirathi from an ice cave at the foot of the Gangotri glacier, 12,770 feet up in the Garhwal Himalayas. The cave is known as Gomukh, the Cow's Mouth; certainly nothing in nature could be nearer the divine than this lonely place to which only the most determined pilgrims used

to penetrate back in the 1960s.

Three hundred miles from its source the Ganges breaks through the Siwalik Range, outriders of the Himalayas, in a gorge a mile wide, and enters the plains of India where the town of Hardwar stands. Spoiled by a number of hideous buildings, some of them plastered with equally hideous advertisements, this is one of the seven great bathing places of pilgrimage in India.

The ghat – steps leading down to the river – is the scene of great bathing ceremonies, especially on the birthday of Ganga, at the beginning of the Hindu solar year, when as many as 400,000 people gather for the bathing, and on the occasion of a Kumbh Mela (a *mela* being a fair), which occurs every twelfth year when the planet Jupiter is in Aquarius (Kumbh), the bathers are said to number millions.

Here, and everywhere else on the banks of the Ganges, the bathers can be seen engaged in various acts of reverence to her: drinking her waters, icy in winter; launching small, green, boat-shaped baskets of stitched leaves containing marigolds, rose petals and white sweets, placing them carefully on the water which whirls them about a bit until they are upset and their contents are carried away downstream. There the river winds away, a narrow ribbon of water in the dry seasons, reach after reach of it until it is swallowed up in the haze of the vast plain, a 400,000-square-mile basin formed on the north by the Himalayas, on the south by the Vindhyan Ranges, and to the east where the Brahmaputra enters it, by the thickly forested hills which separate Burma from Bengal. To the west are the great deserts of Rajasthan. In three of the states through which the Ganges flows – Uttar Pradesh, Bihar and West Bengal – lived 190 million people, one

The sandbank full of people at the *Sangam*, Allahabad. The *Sangam* is the place where the Ganges, Jumna and a third, invisible river, the Sarasvati, meet and mingle at what is perhaps the most venerated place of worship in all India. It is *Tirtharaj*, the king among places of worship, which enables human beings who bathe and worship there to cross the ocean of existence and attain salvation.

A bullock cart on the Grand Trunk Road,
Uttar Pradesh.

third of India's entire population.

A hundred miles below Hardwar the river is more or less what it will be for the greater part of the rest of its journey to the Bay of Bengal: a river about two miles wide, narrowing to half a mile or less in winter, then sometimes swollen by the monsoon rains to the proportions of an inland sea.

On the high, right bank, where they are robust enough to resist the encroaching, eroding river, are the permanent villages. It is impossible even to guess at how old they are, for they are built of undatable mud. This is Hindoostan as European artists saw it in the early nineteenth century. Banyan trees grow on the banks, their long branches hanging down like bell-ropes, and, in their shade, the water is the colour of greengages. On top of these banks spindle-shanked men run rather than walk, as such men always do in India, with bamboos slung across their shoulders which have heavy earthenware pots suspended at either end. Sometimes there are men carrying white-wrapped corpses on stretchers to the burning places, crying, 'Ram Nam Sat Hai!' ('The Name of God is Truth!'), followed by the mourners, one of whom is carrying a pot with a fire burning in it. In the river, where there is a shrine, a platform from which a black lingam rises decked with fresh marigolds, some white-clad figures perform their pujas and women and girls wallop the washing on lumps of brickwork – all that remains of some Mughal palace or gazebo – shouting to one another in coarse, cheerful voices. Out on the water there may be ferry boats loaded with men, bicycles and goats, fishing boats loaded with bag-shaped nets, or the cone-shaped traps which are set on the bottom of the river; country boats with upturned bows and square sterns

with a crew of two, some of them being tracked upstream with a tow rope by one man, the other steering. All the way down the river there are *shmasans*, burning places for the dead, often nothing more than a piece of foreshore distinguished by some ashes and calcined bones. The river is full of imperfectly cremated bodies, floating downstream, often with birds of prey using them as rafts, pecking at them.

When the river widens to such an extent that no proper bank is visible, there is nothing but flats and sandbanks on either hand. By night there is pandemonium on these lonely reaches, what with the continual rumble of sandbanks collapsing into them; the noise made by the huge flocks of tall, grey and red sarus cranes as they trumpet and thresh the water; and the howlings of packs of jackals which are taken up and answered by other bands on the opposite bank.

The end – or one of the ends of Ganga, since she has a hundred mouths – is at the southern tip of Sagar Island, where the river meets the Indian Ocean. Here, at the same time as the Mela is celebrated at Hardwar and Allahabad, a great fair attended by many thousands takes place on the shore, lasting three days. Pilgrims used to sacrifice their progeny by offering them to Ganga, which was infested by man-eating estuarine crocodiles (*C. porosus*), and sharks, a practice repressed in 1802 by Lord Wellesley, the Governor-General, after twenty-three people had been either drowned or eaten the previous year.

But it is at the Sandheads, some sixty miles south of Sagar Island, among the dome-shaped sands, invisible twenty fathoms below, where the long trails of sand run down to the deeps of the Indian Ocean and the river in its multiple

guises as Hooghly, Bhagirathi and Ganges deposits on the bottom the dark olive mud mixed with glistening sand that shines like iron filings, the last scourings of a sub-continent, that the Ganga really comes to an end at last.

Overleaf
Bullock carts, which were bogged down, having just crossed a bridge of boats at Raoli, a remote place on the Upper Ganges, south of Hardwar.

Opposite
Opposite
Brahman undergoing massage, Varanasi.

Below
An Aghori outside the Post Office at Benares (Varanasi). Aghoris are believers in Tantric magic, and the ceremony of calling up demons at burning ghats or cemeteries is a typical Tantric rite. They have been described as 'a sect who know no prohibited food', although, it is said, they have an aversion to horse meat.

'If you wish,' said one of the attendants, a fat, indolent fellow at the Tourist Bungalow, 'I am taking you to see one Aghori. He is living at City Post Office. It is a very strange sect. These men are eating their excrements. I am also showing you many other things at Benares, but first I am showing you this man.' At the Post Office we found the Aghori, parked across the entrance, and partly blocking it. It seemed a strange place for a dung eater to hang out. When he realized that we were interested in him, he rolled over to display his sexual organs, which were an impressive size. Among other equipment with which he surrounded himself – old tins, for example, with various disagreeable-looking mixtures in them – was something done up in a cloth that looked as if it might contain his *Mittagessen*. 'I hope it isn't feeding time,' Wanda said.

Below

The car of either the brother or sister of
Jagannath, Lord of the Universe, at Puri,
Orissa – southern India.

Jagannath is a particular form of Vishnu,
the second god of the Hindu Triad, or,
strictly speaking, to make it more complex,
of Krishna. Krishna is said to be the eighth
avatara or incarnation of Vishnu, and is certainly the most popular of Hindu deities.

The great seat of Jagannath worship is the
temple at Puri on the shores of the Bay of
Bengal, originally built in the twelfth century but with many unfortunate subsequent
accretions. Jagannath's enormous popularity

is due to the belief, fostered by succeeding
generations of his attendant priests, that all
castes, however low, are equal before him.
The single most important ceremony con-
cerning Jagannath is when images of him,
his brother Balbhadra and his sister
Subhadra (all roughly carved from tree
trunks, but only Jagannath and his brother
being furnished with arms) are dragged by
4200 followers (whose job this is from year
to year) through the streets to the Gundicha
Mandir, the Garden Temple, on enormous
cars known as *raths*.

Opposite

The Taj Mahal Hotel, Bombay. Last bastion
of the Raj.

Above
Girls bathing at a waterfall, in Orissa, southern India.

Opposite
Children in the street, Madras.

Market Day, which is on Tuesdays, at Hexham, Northumberland.

In Hexham you could buy nailed shepherds' boots and shoes with a slightly turned-up forepart, called the neb, which was supposed to help the wearer over rough ground. There were lighter versions for Sundays. At nearby Corbridge, you could – and still can – have socks made that are virtually unwearoutable. I have several pairs that have lasted for more than twenty years. You can try out these various items on Hadrian's Wall (Wallsend-on-Tyne, Northumberland, to Bowness on Solway, Cumberland, 73 miles), which anywhere else but in Britain would be regarded as one of the Wonders of the World.

One of the best sections is at Mile Castle 30, Limestone Corner on Teppermoor Hill, two and a half miles west of Chollerford on the North Tyne. Here the Roman engineers cut both ditch and vallum through an iron-hard hill composed of quartz dolerite, and huge blocks of the stuff bearing the marks of their wedges can still be seen.

Set in a Silver Sea
Great Britain, 1963

As you come out on Pier Hill at the foot of Southend High Street you get your first smell of the sea, so strong that it is like a biff on the nose. This is what puts Londoners in a good humour, for this is one of the things they have come for – an escape from The Smoke and a whiff of the sea. Or is it mud? Or a mixture of mud and water? Or something else? It is a question one feels entitled to ask. With the tide out the nearest sea is a mile away. If there is fog in Sea Reach you may not even be able to see it. Whatever it is, it has a strong maritime flavour, and it is best to make the most of it as it is certainly the best smell you're going to smell while you're here.

The smell and, on a fine day, the sight of the sea make the journey worthwhile, because seawards there is always something going on. In 1962 the Signal Station at the end of the pier reported 53,209 vessels to Lloyd's. For this reason, if no other, Southend has the edge on Blackpool. It is not one of those places where the visitor gazes despairingly at the horizon longing for a puff of smoke to break the monotony.

See Southend on a fine Saturday morning any time from June to October. If the tide is out the cockle boats will be on their sides, stranded. Out towards the North Sea, off Shoeburyness, a line of tankers is waiting for the tide; beyond them the Great Nore Tower is like a cluster of skeletal birds up to their knee joints in water. After early rain the sky is the colour of pearls. Sea, mud and sky merge into one another. The atmosphere is the sort from which mirages are made. If there wasn't the pier with the statue of Queen Victoria pointing lugubriously down it, as if banishing you to govern New South Wales, it would be difficult to tell where the elements begin and end.

Three miles across the estuary is the Kentish shore, and places with lovely names – All Hallows, St Mary's Hoo, Sheppey, the Isle of Grain: not all of them so lovely now. Between Grain and Sheppey three Thames sailing barges are anchored: another, with a gaff topsail set and flying a red burgee with a white crescent on it, is beating down channel. The scene lacks only a great fish stranded on one of the banks and it might be a drawing by the elder Brueghel.

All the way from London, unless you travel by the arterial road, you have tantalizing glimpses of ships and water, the widening reaches of the river. On the old Southend Road in the no-man's-land beyond Dagenham, part country, part desert, where the chimneys of the cement factories point sad fingers to the sky, Southend begins to put its spell on you. Around half past ten the coaches with outings on board – beanos as old cockle sellers on the front still call them – draw into the lay-bys – great glossy monsters with incongruously sylvan names like Bluebell and Primrose. The beer crates and the big jars of pickled onions are unloaded from the boot and the beanos themselves cluster round the crates, rather solemn-looking, as though they were taking part in a ritual, which in a sense they are.

These are all-male beanos, mostly

Desert Rat vintage or even earlier, going back as far as Passchendaele. There are mixed coachloads and whole coachloads of girls and coaches full of old ladies, but they stop at different lay-bys, with amenities, and they don't have beer and onions. They have more ladylike refreshments, mostly, and make themselves comfortable for the final run in.

If you travel on the *Royal Sovereign* or the *Royal Daffodil* from Tower Pier you have water all the way, plus the smell of engine room and beer in the bars; but in addition you will have seen strange, isolated places which, like me, you may have planned to go to, brooding over ordnance maps in the loo on winter evenings, but never reached because when you have the time the Dolomites seem nearer. The seventeenth-century fort at Tilbury that one would certainly have been to long before if it had been in France; the Isolation Hospital on the marshes at Lower Hope, surrounded by wire, waiting for a solitary Lascar with smallpox or a Dutchman off a boat from the Indies – ideal setting for a play by Dürrenmatt; and the marshes themselves, places on which, during the war, they exploded nasty things where now the sheep nibble the grass under a cat's cradle of grid lines, the sound of the bell buoys tolling mournfully in the stream over the dyke accentuating their loneliness.

Land on the pier and you instantly become a statistic, albeit a misleading one. In 1962, according to the official report, 246,025 people landed and embarked on Southend Pier, of whom 123,012 are 'presumed' to have become visitors. Before you leave for the shore, see for yourself what happened to the missing 123,013. You will find them on the sun deck laid out in orderly rows, cheek by jowl in deck chairs. The majority are elderly, which may account for nobody having worried about them before. Although they are not the sort of people who would make beasts of themselves with pickled onions in lay-bys, you will find them all hard at work eating. They eat silently and continuously. Most of them are eating a rather indigestible-looking sugar bun, like a lightly cooked sausage with a coating of shaving cream on it.

You cannot visit Southend without sampling the shellfish at one or other of the numberless booths at the entrance to the pier. Study the price lists, by all means, but they all seem to be the same. Oysters don't look so good? Try the whelks. Rather like chewing India-rubber bone. (Who organizes the retail price maintenance of whelks?) Whilst champing, consider the merits of a whelk tea, also on offer. But allow me to warn you: the effect of strong tea on whelks is similar to the effect of whisky on oysters, which is no good at all.

Right
Dunnottar Castle, Kincardineshire. A very craggy, ruinous ruin two miles south of Stonehaven, separated by a gorge from the mainland and perched 160 feet up on a rock. During the wars of the Commonwealth, the Scottish Royal Regalia was kept here, and the crown and sceptre were carried out through the lines to the church at Kineff, six miles to the south, by the wife of the minister there. They were hidden behind the pulpit.

Lots of atmosphere existed here years ago, and may indeed still exist, providing the castle has not been tarted up, or made to form part of a 'nature trail'.

Overleaf
McCaig's Folly.

I love follies. We have had two in our lives, a Gothick grotto and now an obelisk. McCaig's Folly looms over the town of Oban in Argyll. Built of granite in about 1900 by a Mr John Stuart McCaig, banker, self-styled art critic and philosophical essayist, it is a copy of the Colosseum in Rome in comparatively midget form – 200 feet in diameter, up to 47 feet in height, with two tiers of pointed arches, 50 on the top tier, 44 on the bottom. Mr McCaig planned to have a tower rising, rocketlike, from its centre, but, as with all the best folly fanciers, his aspirations were never completely realized.

Fine as McCaig's Folly is, it cannot begin to emulate Scotland's first folly – the Dunmore Pineapple, a 50-foot-high summer house in the form of a pineapple, in the grounds of Dunmore Castle in Stirlingshire.

Below

Wistman's Wood, Dartmoor, an ancient, wind-blasted wood of dwarf oaks, 1300 feet up, on the side of the valley of the West Dart. It is one of three surviving such copses on the moor. The trees grow from crevices between moss-covered rocks. It is a weird, wonderful place. Another, less well-known, is Black Tor Beare, between 1200 and 1500 feet up on the bank of the West Okement River, under Black Tor, east of Sourton.

Opposite

Clytha Castle (in Monmouthshire when I photographed it). This magnificent folly is on the edge of a grove of what were then truly gigantic chestnut, beech and cedar trees. It had round and square towers, a curtain wall that rose at the centre as if draped, topped with a miniature turret, mysterious locked and studded doors; and inside, a densely overgrown courtyard. Built by an eighteenth-century gentleman to alleviate the sadness caused by the death of his wife, it seemed to hold within it all the melancholy which he had worked so hard to expunge. It has since been done up.

A Queen's Ransom

Crossing the Atlantic, 1965 and 1972

'WHAT is it about being on a boat that makes everyone behave like a film star?' Lady Julia Mottram (née Flyte) asks Charles Ryder in Evelyn Waugh's *Brideshead Revisited*, while crossing the Atlantic in one of the Cunard *Queens* between the wars. She had just, against all common sense, settled for a bout below deck with a hefty *masseuse*.

If Ryder had recorded his answer, it would probably have been to the effect that scarcely ever, except on a transatlantic liner, are there four days and a half with absolutely nothing to do except summon up a massager, spend the morning entombed under a mud-pack, or have one's toes seen to. It was still true in 1965 of the *Queen Mary* and the *Queen Elizabeth* and, in descending order of size, of the *France*, the United States Line's *United States*, the Italia Line's *Raffaello*, the Holland-Amerika Line's *Rotterdam* and the Norddeutscher Lloyd's *Bremen*.

To travel in the *Queen Elizabeth*, as we did, from New York to Southampton, was an experience. There were ships that were far more modern, but there would never be another in which there was so much space. It had 37 public rooms, some of them three decks high and rather overpowering. It had three acres of deck. It had one open-air and two indoor swimming pools. The open-air pool, like the teenage room, was a daring innovation, the legacy of a recent refit. It had a Turkish bath, staffed by a squad of men and women who would knock hell out of you for a consideration, just as

their predecessors had beaten it out of Lady Julia.

Altogether, there were 12 bars on the *Queen Elizabeth*, some of them impossible to find without help in the space of an average crossing of 4 days 13 hours. There were two gymnasiums equipped with weird cast-iron machines built with bits of bicycles that brought to mind the Marx Brothers on their transatlantic crossing with Margaret Dumont. There were two cinemas. And there were kennels for 26 four-footed friends (once they conveyed a deodorized skunk).

There were operating theatres and little rooms equipped with live stenographers to help you get on with your business. And somewhere on board there must have been a garden, because there was a gardener. There was even a squash court which must have been a pretty hazardous place until they equipped the ship with stabilizers.

The decor of most of the public rooms resembled that of a 1930s country house designed for Lord Beaverbrook: all panelled with petula, patapsko pomla, avodire, tiger oak, makore, bubinga, zebrano and black bean, woods which no one but a timber merchant had ever heard of, much less seen. One half-expected to meet Garbo, wearing a turban, marching up one of the countless grand staircases for an assignation with John Barrymore to the strains of music played by the Marcel Torrens Palm Court Orchestra in the Main Lounge, Reginald Foort on the organ. If you were too young to know what the thirties were like, the *Queen Eliza-*

Last view of old New York from Le Bon Bateau *France* in 1972, just as if the architect of the World Trade Center was about to shut the sliding doors on it. To build these colossi, he had 1.2 million yards of earth and rock excavated from Manhattan Island and dumped in the Hudson. Lucky we didn't run aground.

beth was the ship to travel in. Even the First Class suites had as much chintz and as many doors as a bedroom in an Aldwych farce, and the plumbing was of a solidity and splendour matched at that time only by that of the North British Hotel, Edinburgh, which had been installed in Edwardian times.

The service was terrific. Men wearing rows of medal ribbons stood all day by lifts which some passenger might conceivably decide to use. Many of the stewards had been stewarding for forty years. Unlike the French with their *France*, such men as these were not given a prize at the end of the year by their government to encourage them to fresh heights of service and affability. It came from the heart, and by the time we had tipped them in the manner to which they were accustomed there was no need for such incentives. (Cunard, unlike P & O, for example, didn't publish a list of suggested tips for the guidance of passengers such as ourselves.)

These men and the stewardesses would do anything for you – well, almost anything – and if you had an overwhelming desire to eat buttered toast at 4.30 a.m., eat it you could, and uncongealed. They were all things to all men and women: matey without being impertinent in Tourist Class, reserved in Cabin Class; while in First Class they had the air of privilege of a family butler, which was why to multitudes of well-off Americans who travelled in the *Queen Elizabeth* it was a foretaste of what they believed to be the British way of life, perhaps the only part of their visit to Britain which really lived up to their expectations.

It was the food by which such a ship was ultimately judged, and if you were so minded you could eat your way into an untimely grave (there were no burials at sea). In Tourist Class the food was copious and wholesome; in Cabin Class it came from the same kitchens as First Class, but they were less reckless with such commodities as caviar, which, in First, came up in big dollops. The First Class breakfast menu listed more than ninety separate items, including onion soup, fried yellow perch, cold roast lamb and mint sauce (we never actually saw anyone eating this), eight different coffees and fourteen different kinds of bread.

If all this was insufficient to see you through until lunchtime, a deck steward would swaddle you in a red and blue blanket, like a great baby, and feed you beef tea from 11 a.m. onwards. The blanket was the best refuge from those tedious amusements which flourished on all passenger ships, such as bean-guessing and funny hat competitions, and still do.

For an extra ten bob you could eat in the Verandah Grill. Just as the Royal Enclosure at Ascot had other more select enclosures within it, on a *Queen* there was always another restaurant that was classier than the First Class. In it you could order almost anything, from Westphalian ham to bouillabaisse, and get it. You could order entirely black meals, starting with caviar and ending with Finnish black pudding eaten with blackcurrant jam, or entirely white meals of boiled fish, tripe and junket. We met an English lawyer and his wife who were eating their way through all the puddings they had not eaten since they were in the nursery – spotted dog, treacle pud., jam sponge, and so on. All were delicious. They ought to have been. These were the dishes the crew liked best and there were 1190 crew members to just over 2000 passengers.

* * *

By 1972 both the *Queens* were out of commission and the largest liner in the world was the *France* (66,348 tons), taken into service in 1962 by the *Compagnie Générale Transatlantique* (English alias, the French Line). When we sailed in her from New York to Southampton, she had just completed a three-month, one-class, round-the-world winter cruise, which ended in New York. All 1200 berths were occupied. On this marathon an outside cabin on U deck (*luxe*) cost £5920, and the most expensive suite, £30,000 (*grande luxe*), for four passengers. Among the two thousand passengers on 'our' crossing there were no readily identifiable film stars, but there was M. Salvador Dali, carrying a sort of wand and looking like a cross between a necromancer and *Le Roi Soleil*. There was also a cross-section of an entire Arabian royal family, attempting, with total lack of success, to cross the Atlantic incognito in a couple of dozen upper-deck cabins, complete with their own coffee makers, bodyguards, veiled houris, servants whose feet were killing them, and lots of children and *au pairs*. In addition the ship was awash with American millionaires, as such ships always were in the autumn, who were always sloping off to the Tourist Class Night Club because they said it was more fun. At Southampton they were met by a whole fleet of Daimler hire cars in which they purred away to the Connaught and Claridge's. There was even a small parcel of distinguished savants.

How did this heterogeneous collection manage to while away the not-so-long days and nights? Well, we whiled them away swimming in one or other of the two swimming pools (a notice on D deck informed us that the water was heated to some agreeable tropical temperature, but all we found was raw Atlantic

straight from the ocean). We were massaged, being older now and more in need of it than we had been on the *Queen Elizabeth*, had haircuts and, of course, pedicures. There was also ping-pong, bowling, a shooting gallery, dance lessons, a library of six thousand volumes, and an outpost of the *Galeries Lafayette*, which advised all First Class passengers to come in the afternoon 'so that they will enjoy the best service'.

We tried both First and Tourist Class service and found the assistants equally rude and disobliging in both, the only people we encountered in the entire ship out of a crew of 1100 who were rude and disobliging, but then they weren't members of the crew.

We could also go to the cinema in the biggest theatre afloat, ride a mechanical horse in the gym (a surprisingly obscene-looking machine), dial 1900 for dollops of bad news – there was also a daily paper – or give up completely, as most transatlantiqueurs eventually do, and allow ourselves to be swaddled in wrappings by the deck stewards and left to mature like Tutankhamun. Someone on board had brought with them a cougar or an ocelot, I can't remember which. It was kept on deck, in what were intended as dog kennels, equipped with French lamp posts and kilometre stones. One wondered what it made of them and the other four-footed friends.

Most popular of all the distractions were the bars – the one in Tourist Class was 69 feet long and said to be the longest in the maritime world. The *Bar d'Atlantique* in First Class was presided over by M. Raymond Cordier, archpriest of transatlantic barmen and most agreeable of men, who had been forty years with the company, ten in the *France*. He made what were arguably the finest Bloody Marys in the world, and

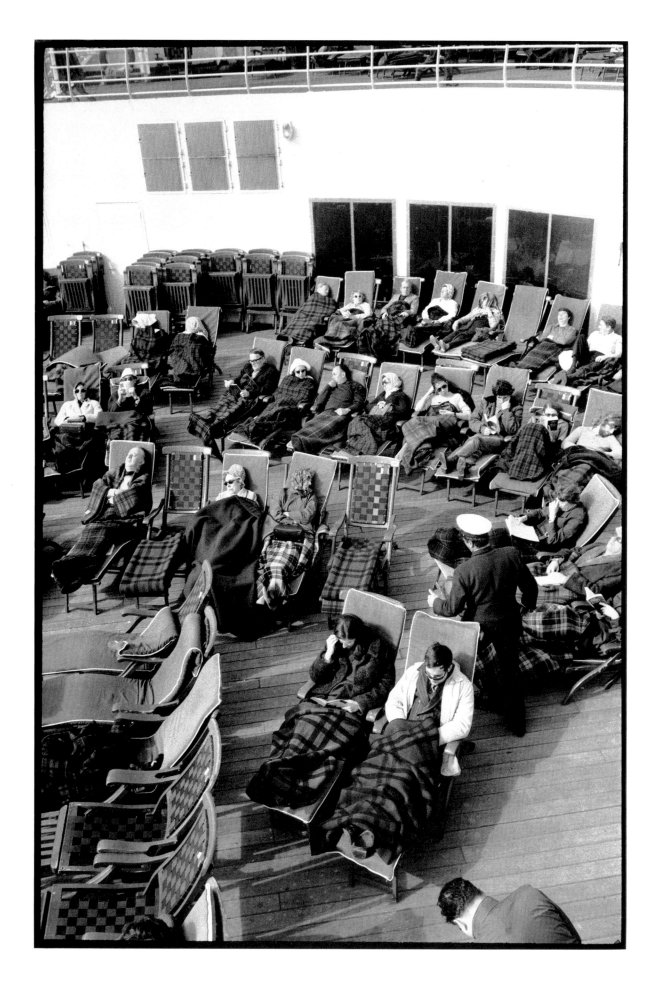

never spilt a drop of liquor other than down his customers' throats.

What many people came for, rather than to gaze at the ocean, or ride a mechanical horse, was the food. Breakfast was a sort of litany, as in the *Queen Elizabeth*, with nine different sorts of jam. But it's what we didn't eat that we remember. Looking at the menus today I wonder why I never had Pickled Herring in Chablis, Medallion of Huachinango Sauté Concarnoise, Broiled Rock Cornish Hen Saint-Germain (animal, veg. or mineral?), or a Religieuse with Coffee. At the Captain's Dinner, which was followed by *Le Dancing*, there was Bird's Nest Soup.

Nevertheless, partly because the *France* was unable to replenish its store with fresh eggs in New York for the last lap to Southampton, the palm for food must be given to the *Queen Elizabeth*. The *France* was more sophisticated but, oddly enough, less fun. At Southampton, while queuing for immigration, we heard one well-heeled English person say to another: 'I'll telephone *my* butler and tell him to telephone *your* butler and say we need *both* Rolls.'

Sun deck of the *France*, around 11 a.m. in mid-Atlantique. There wasn't much sun, but very soon stewards would arrive, and, after ascertaining by holding a mirror to their lips that the recumbent forms were in the land of the living, they would offer those with British passports beef tea, and those with US passports some French equivalent, such as *Le Bullshot*.

Belle and bicyclist in Rue Mably, Bordeaux, 1968.

Behind the waterfront of this beautiful city, on a great bend of the Garonne, five miles of *quais* with ugly sheds on them obscured what had been a river frontage of eighteenth-century houses, whose lower parts had been converted into tiny bars which, at night, were packed tight with tight sailors. To a person with my kind of imagination, some of the old and decrepit streets behind looked positively sinister, but no doubt they were innocuous enough.

Outside the Romanesque church of Ste Croix in Place Prenaudel, tramps or *chiffonniers* (rag-and-bone men), of whom there were large numbers at that time in Bordeaux, sat with pramloads of what were either their possessions or junk watching boys playing *boules*. The next morning they could be seen hovering around the early morning fires in the flea market in Place Mériadeck.

Travels in the Cévennes
Without a Donkey
France, 1965

Tuesday A fine, windy crossing to Calais. Drove to Boulogne to find that night train to Avignon could not accommodate vehicles over 64½ inches in height. Land Rover 77½ inches. Forced to remove entire metal superstructure with spanners. Left with huge piles of nuts, struts and bolts, side windows, etc., like jumbo-size Meccano set. Shared couchette with family of five. Carriages very new with clean towels. The train left at 8.10 p.m.

Wednesday Arrived Avignon 8.20 a.m. Vehicles unloaded at rural siding complete with snack bar and wash place. French officials all trying to win courtesy prize.

Exhausted by rebuilding Land Rover we spent rest of the morning under plane trees in Place de l'Horloge. How expensive it became sitting under plane trees in Place de l'Horloge!

Crossed Rhône in sizzling midday heat; through gravelly wastes to Tavel. Drank excellent, cold Tavel rosé in deserted main square. Then through the Forêts de Tavel and Malmont, strange, stony, almost waterless wastes, peppered with ilex and dwarf oaks and scented with thyme and lavender. Ate very good *charcuterie* in the ink-pot black shade of an ilex tree and finished the other half of the still-cold Tavel, to the insane music of *cigales*.

5 p.m. Alès, dreary industrial town on the Gardon d'Alès, a river which has almost as many branches as our bank. R. L. Stevenson came here after travelling with and selling his donkey, Modestine, but only to collect his mail.

By winding, wooded D 50. Saw forest of giant bamboos, 20 metres high, in Parc de Prafance. With sun going down rapidly, drove along wooded valley of another Gardon, Gardon de Mialet, and stopped at a fine, unofficial-looking camp site in a grove of chestnut trees down by the river, beyond Le Mialet. Fearful job pegging down tent on iron-hard soil using alloy pegs which behaved like folding teaspoons from a joke shop. The farm had some likely-looking chickens raised on good farmyard grit running about. Wanda ordered one for the following day. She then cooked veal in wine. Slept soundly on punctured airbed.

Thursday Very hot morning – tent like an oven. Re-pitched it under a tree. Magnificent swimming in deep pools. Thousands of butterflies. Collected blackberries. Dined on chicken cooked with thyme, ratatouille, blackberries in wine, and drank Tavel rosé. Afterwards went for black-as-pitch swim in the Gardon. At 3 a.m. heard weird noises outside tent. Shades of Dominici and the dead Drummonds? Finally, I emerged trouserless from the tent armed with a hammer, whereupon the noises ceased.

Friday Warm and beautiful day. To St Jean du Gard, little town with one long street where Stevenson sold his donkey. Outside the town bought the most delicious honey we had ever tasted – as black as treacle.

Then through great, wooded mountains, past deserted villages and abandoned terrace fields to the mouth of the Tunnel du Marquaires, which burrows through the Cévennes watershed. This was the divide for the weather, too. Overhead it was as if the master chef was stirring a *pot au feu*. From it a long descent to Racoules on the Tarnon where there was a pleasant-looking camping place and an equally pleasant little inn close by.

Then on down the Tarnon to the little town of Florac at its junction with the Tarn, with the cliffs of the high plateau of the Causse Méjean (*causse* being a high plateau) looming over it – a good place for shopping but too many cars (even in 1965). Then up the Tarn, now very beautiful and peaceful with many unorganized places for camping which you would not be allowed to use today; and then up the valley of the Mirals river with heather-covered hills rising above it.

Here, we met a young woman who said we could camp down by the river, where there was a water meadow with apple trees growing in it. Hidden under a cliff, there was a disused mill house with the date 1718 over the door, built with huge blocks of stone, the interior all shrouded in cobwebs.

Weather now very threatening, with clouds like giant black puffballs dead overhead. Pitched tent on little mound in the water meadow. No point in being washed away. In the mill house Wanda cooked duck in wine, ratatouille from previous evening and stewed blackberries with windfall apples, followed by a goat cheese from a village at the head of the valley. Fine if you like goat's cheese.

Saturday Woke to find that the mound with the tent on it was now an island. Waded to mill for breakfast. Then set off on foot in showery weather up the steep side of a ridge between the valleys of the Mirals and the Briançon. Strong wind at the top. To the southwest black rain clouds were pouring over the edge of the Causse Méjean. Deep down below us, in the valley of the Briançon, there was a minute village, its houses built of brown stone and with slate roofs, now shiny with rain. Higher up, the tributaries of the Briançon reached up to stony crests like long green veins and to the east-northeast the Mirals fell away into the valley in a long, white plume; while from north to south the Cévennes rose and fell, more like a rough sea than a mountain range.

We climbed round the head of a valley to a village set amongst tor-like rocks. Inside the houses, some of which had only recently been abandoned, there were fireplaces with cowled chimney pieces, huge dressers, old cordial bottles bearing the names of long-extinct firms, mid-nineteenth-century religious books and tracts (the people in this region were ardent Protestants), calendars of the 1900s, little round boxes full of buttons, old coats with braided lapels and suits of velveteen (one with a family of mice living in its pockets) and, upstairs, mounds of bedding, all surprisingly clean, mountain boots and strange wardrobes that resembled the bodies of old stage coaches.

Every house was deserted, except one. Inside it a woman of fifty or sixty was sitting by an open fire. She and her husband were the last occupants. Before the last war forty people had lived here. She was lonely, she said, but she didn't like towns or cities.

A white-washed rock, part of the mountain, protruded into the room. In one corner there was a big double bed. Homemade sausages hung from hooks in the ceiling. Outside, on a wooden platform, undercover, was all their gear: saws, felling axes and sledges for bringing the wood in from the forests.

Back at the camp we ate sausages made with herbs, beans with oil and vinegar, goat's cheese and a fruit tart bought in Florac.

Sunday An impressive, windswept dawn, then rain. Breakfast was scrambled eggs, stewed apples, bread and the black honey.

Then we climbed to one of the villages we had seen the previous day. Only three houses were occupied in this one. Some of the children had curious pop-eyes.

After this, in the Land Rover, up the road which ran alongside the main stream of the Briançon, passing gleaming water meadows, irrigated by little ditches which ran along the hillsides like creeping plants, and up the screes of Mont Lozère where broom grew and huge thistles which the local people nailed to the doors of their houses as barometers (they closed when it was going to rain).

A starry night. Very cold. Wanda cooked, or rather re-heated, a guinea fowl cooked that morning, bought because of a shortage of chickens. Like a lot of guinea fowl this one was a bit rubbery but the gravy was good.

Monday Up the right bank of the Tarn to Le Pont de Montvert, a small, windy village at the meeting of several valleys. Here we bought wine from barrels in a barrel-shaped cellar and homemade ice cream.

Then on up to the Col de Finiels on open downs on Mont Lozère, as lonely as the loneliest parts of the Cheviots, where the wind was tearing the sky apart and one solitary shepherd in an immense green canvas cloak stood alone with his sheep in this vast landscape as if he was the last shepherd on earth. Until recently the Causses had been treeless, huge expanses of rock and stones with minimal quantities of earth in which thin grass, lavender, marjoram, wild thyme and dozens of other herbs grew. Nevertheless they supported vast flocks of sheep.

Every year, in the spring, the sheep were walked up from Bas-Languedoc by their shepherds to the Causses and Mont Lozère in the Cévennes by way of *les drailles*, paths on which, at intervals of a day's journey, there were huts and pens for the accommodation of the shepherds and their sheep. In the autumn the journey was made in reverse. This was the *transhumance*. The wool from these sheep was used for making French Army uniforms.

Now the government was embarking on a huge programme of tree-planting on the Causses that would transform it, in much the same way as Fabre had done in the Cévennes in the 1870s to replace the beech forests cut down by charcoal burners and ravaged by goats. This reafforestation was naturally unpopular with the shepherds of the Causses and mysterious acts of arson had already taken place.

To walk along the ridge of Mont Lozère from end to end must be, I thought at the time, one of the great walks of the world. One day, I promised myself, I would do it, but I have not done so yet.

Overleaf
St-Emilion, Gironde. A vineyard village built of golden limestone, a lot of it subterranean, in one of the most beautiful situations in all France (in my opinion, that is). During the Revolution it became the last refuge of those luckless moderates, the *Girondins*.

Below

Sunday morning on the pavement of Rue Thomas, Marché aux Puces de Bicêtre, Paris. Outside the Porte d'Italie – nearest Métro, Kremlin-Bicêtre.

In the realms of flea markets it would have been difficult to find a much more flea-ridden flea market, or one less contrived for the tourist than this one. The *exposants* brought their offerings to the site in every imaginable and unimaginable form of transport, from perambulators to hearses, and laid them out for one's delectation under the trees on Sundays and Tuesday and Thursday mornings. The Bicêtre was more or less the end of the road from the point of view of the commodities on offer, and even if you got there on the dot when it opened at 6 a.m. on Sunday mornings, you would be lucky to find a doll's head of the sort shown in this picture, and might have to content yourself with a cardboard boxful of reject brassieres, or a ditto full of old radio valves. Whatever the commodity, however, and no matter how awful its condition, the owners put such an exaggerated value on it that it was almost impossible to conclude any business deals at all.

Opposite

Much better, and, in the late 1950s, not often frequented by tourists, was the Marché aux Puces at St Ouen, out beyond the Porte de Clignancourt, Paris – nearest Métro, Porte de Clignancourt. There, in the part of the market known as Paul-Bert (there are eight principal divisions), we bought for £10 a long case provincial clock of the sort that every farmhouse in France used to have in its kitchen, and many still do. The current price is around £800 for one in similar condition. We brought it back to Dover in the back of a short-based Land Rover from which it protruded several feet. There the customs authorities, suspecting that it was a coffin with a corpse in it, made us unload it.

Jerusalem. An Orthodox Jew at the Wall, the Kothel ma'arvi, the Wailing Place of the Jews. This section of the western wall of the Second Temple is fifty yards long, sixty feet and twenty-four courses high (with sixteen more courses invisible below the surface). Orthodox Jews come to bemoan the downfall of their Temple, the destruction of their City and the Diaspora, the dispersal of their race. It is also sacred to Muslims, being part of the wall of the Harām es-Sherif, the Place of the Temple, where Mohammed tethered his mare, al-Burak, after his miraculous overnight ride from Mecca.

Not Such a Promising Land

Israel, 1965

JERUSALEM in February 1965 was a bit chilly, not surprisingly as it is 2500 feet up in the air on a bare, almost waterless, limestone plateau. How King David, a thousand years before Christ, came to choose such a site for his capital, having captured it from the inoffensive Jebusites, is a bit of a mystery. One of his reasons must have been because it was isolated, and therefore, he hoped, free from corrupting, outside influences, something that would have been inescapable down on the shores of the Mediterranean, thirty miles or so away, where every ship that arrived was a possible harbinger of innovation and change.

At that time, in 1965, the New City, which was being developed by the Israelis, was entirely sealed off from the Old City, which was still in Jordanian territory. It was a state of affairs that benefited neither side, but one that was to become even worse for the Jordanians two years later, in 1967, when they were thrown out completely.

There was something decidedly eerie about one's first sight of the battlemented western wall of Jordanian-occupied Old Jerusalem, pierced by the then blocked-up Jaffa Gate, one of the seven gates of the city, all of which, well into the twentieth century, were shut at night, leaving anyone still outside the walls at the mercy of marauding Beduin. This was the gate used by the victorious General Allenby when, on 11 December 1917, having received the Turkish surrender, he entered the city on foot.

Next to it there was a large hole in the wall, also now blocked up, made by order of Sultan Abd ul-Hamid II, so that Kaiser Wilhelm II, dressed in shining armour, could ride into the city on a white horse in order to attend the consecration of the Lutheran Church of the Redeemer.

It was eerie because all frontiers by their nature are eerie, and because on this one there was no sign of life, except where the sun caught the field glasses of a sentry in one of the Jordanian look-out posts. It was like some gigantic filmset from which the extras had departed.

Just to the south of Allenby Square, where the Israeli houses nestled close under the walls, the little streets were either sealed off at one end or else were placarded 'Danger!' 'Frontier Ahead!' It was here that the real no-man's-land began. It led southward down along the foot of the west wall, past David's Tower and down to the Pool of the Sultan, rebuilt in the sixteenth century by Suleiman the Magnificent as a reservoir for rainwater on the site of an earlier pool, at which Crusaders used to water their horses.

To the west of this pool, facing the walls on the side of the valley, was the first suburb of the New Jerusalem (Yemin-Moshe, otherwise Miskenot Sha'ananim, the 'Home of the Unworried'), the first Jewish settlement outside the walls of the Old City. Fort-like houses were built here, at the top end of the Vale of Hinnom, by the English Jewish philanthropist Sir Moses Montefiore, while Palestine was still under Turkish rule, to encourage Jews to leave the confines of the Old City and

create a new life outside the walls. In the alleys of Yemin-Moshe, huge-eyed children played hopscotch and tip-cat.

Above that was the Central Railway Station, terminus of the line from Tel Aviv, built by the Turks in 1892, the first railway line in the Middle East. Below it the Vale of Hinnom curled away downhill round the southern wall of the Old City; only the upper part was in Israeli territory. Above it was Mount Zion, in a salient of the frontier, close to the southwest corner of the walled city and separated from it and the Gate of Zion by a no-man's-land of Armenian and Latin burial grounds, to be glimpsed furtively through bullet holes in rusty iron doors.

Here, on the Mount, outside the present wall, within a labyrinth of courts, was the stone tomb of David, venerated by Muslims, too, on which rested the great silver crowns of the Torah, the Law. The work of building this last wall took five years and the Sultan Suleiman had the builder in charge put to death for omitting to include within it what was for long presumed to be, but some boring experts now say isn't, the burial place of David. Whether it is or is not, and it would have been very difficult to persuade any practising Jew that it wasn't, Jews still came here, grasping the railings that separated it from the rest of the small room in which it stood. During the years when they were denied access to the Wailing

Above
Jerusalem. An inhabitant of Me'a She'arim – member of an ultra-orthodox central or eastern European sect – entering a synagogue. Me'a She'arim means 'hundred fold', and is derived from the text in Genesis, 'Then Isaac sowed in that land and received in the same year a hundred fold and the land blessed him'. Photography is not encouraged in Me'a She'arim, and anyone driving a car in its vicinity on the Sabbath is likely to have it stoned.

Opposite
Sinai, 1971. The favourite wife of Sheikh el Sheikh Abu Abdullah of the Umzeini Beduin, photographed while travelling in then dangerous country occupied by Egyptian infiltrators, with a heavily armed escort. She was photographed by Wanda, the only one of our party allowed near her. While the rest of the harem travelled in black tent-like litters on camel-back, she sat in the front of a very smart jeep, next to the driver.

Wall, they used to come here to pray in large numbers.

A few years ago, in the mid-1980s, you could walk round the walls of Jerusalem on every side except the east, where the Golden Gate was, and where the Muslim burial grounds are above the Valley of the Kidron, opposite the Mount of Olives. Twenty-five years or so ago, if you had been an Arab and had exposed your noddle near the western section of the Wall, an Israeli sniper on the other side of the Hebron Road would have drilled a hole in it. The situation today again looks decidedly unpromising.

Tuarah Beduin camel racing. Sinai, 1971, under Israeli occupation.
    When the Tuarah pray, they turn to a whitewashed tomb on a low hill in which the remains of a notable saint, Nebih Salih, are interred, instead of to Mecca. When we were there, his green silk turban, together with some offerings – a tin-opener, some pieces of mirror, a plastic bag – had been placed on the coffin. At one time the tomb was embellished with more picturesque objects; ostrich eggs, shawls, halters and bridles, but no more.

Jebeliyeh children in Wadi Shuaib, Sinai, 1971.

When the Monastery of St Katharine was founded in AD 530 at the foot of Mount Sinai, the Mountain of the Law, by order of the Byzantine Emperor Justinian I, on the site where the Burning Bush grew, he pro-vided it with a staff of slaves, some of whom were Egyptian, some Christians from Wallachia (a region of southern Rumania). They were known as Jebeliyeh, People of the Mountain. Although the last of the Christian Jebeliyeh, a woman, died in 1740, and they are now all Muslims, they are still looked down upon by the Beduin of the peninsula as Nazarenes (Christians) and *fellahin* (peasants). As to whether they look like Wallachians, who, unless they have seen a Wallachian, can say?

Castles in the Air

Spain, 1965

BACK in 1965, for those who wanted to pass a week or two in wild country among pastoral people there was scarcely anywhere in Europe to compare with the Picos de Europa in the north of Spain, the mountainous area on the borders of Santander, Asturias and Leon (the actual place where these provinces meet is on the 7710-foot Pico Tesorero right in the middle of the massif).

The peaks rose in pale clusters like giant fungi. They are not particularly high but they are sheer, and standing in the heart of them it was difficult to believe that you were only about fifteen miles from the sea. In clear weather they shimmered remotely in a haze of heat; in bad weather, when the clouds pressed down on their tops, they seemed to take a step forward and close in on the narrow valleys. This was when they were at their most awe-inspiring, when the clouds swirled down through the gullies, and from high above came the sound of falling rocks and stones.

Up here in the Picos, even if one had no intention of climbing them but only of scrambling about between them, it was wise to be properly equipped. There were a number of mountain refuges for climbers and skiers. The wild life was extensive, much of the area was a National Park. There were chamois, known locally as the *rebeco*, which had been saved from extinction by the intervention of King Alfonso XIII at a time when they were rapidly being exterminated in great *battues*.

There were wolves, wild cats, eagle owls, eagles and ospreys; and it was also one of the refuges of the European Brown Bear, the flesh of which the inhabitants used to smoke-cure like ham. It is therefore not surprising that in 1989 little more than half a dozen remain. The Picos were as remote in their way as the mountains of the Hindu Kush on the borders of Nuristan, and they bore a remarkable resemblance to them.

The inhabitants existed in an isolation that was truly remarkable. Many of the villages were snowed up for half the year. One of the most lonely was in a cleft at the foot of an enormous cliff and in winter it must have lain in almost perpetual shadow. The only way to it was by a narrow path which corkscrewed up to it through a gorge, and it was a wonder that anyone in the second half of the twentieth century still had the resolution to live there.

The people of the Picos were short, dark, and round-headed. In summer they made a powerful and excellent cheese from goat's milk, curdled by having a calf's gall put into it, called Picon, which at its best resembled a decaying Roquefort. The bad feeling that had always existed between the people of the remote village of Sotres and the equally remote village of Tresviso was all about whose cheese was the best. Both sorts smelt terrible and it needed strength of mind to bring one home to England.

They also made butter which they stored, together with the cheese, in stone bothies. When they had made enough to warrant a journey to one of the surrounding valleys, the black-robed women (some of the older

A woman of the Picos de Europa on her way down to a village, four thousand feet below, to sell or barter a load of butter. She would accomplish the journey, fifteen miles there and back, in one single day.

109

ones wore green petticoats trimmed with orange or scarlet) loaded the butter and cheese on to ponies and travelled fifteen miles down the mountainside at a murderous lope to a village, where they either sold or bartered it. They accomplished the thirty-mile journey, which included a four-thousand-foot descent and ascent, in one day.

When travelling without animals they carried packs made from a whole goatskin; wearing them with the forelegs over their shoulders and the hind legs around the waist, they appeared to have animals crouching on their backs, like figures in a painting by Hieronymous Bosch. It was a strange sight.

This region was already in danger, in 1965, of suffering the same fate as the Italian Dolomites. Roads were planned up the deep valleys of the Duje river to Sotres, and up the Cares, which had splendid salmon fishing at that time, to the village of Cain. A *teleférico* was already under construction which would take tourists 2000 metres up into the Picos from Fuento-Dé, where the river Deva rose. Perhaps the people of Tresviso, Sotres and Cain would be glad. For them this was no mountain arcady. They would probably soon be happily selling souvenirs, but a way of life would be gone for ever. Now, in 1989, what was feared for the Picos and its inhabitants has come true.

Below
Women in the remote village of Sotres in the Picos de Europa, returning from the fields. The leading woman is carrying a pack made from a whole goatskin.

Opposite
Pilgrims in the Plaza Alfonso outside the cathedral in Santiago de Compostela, in Galicia, northwest Spain.

The remains of St James the Greater, beheaded in Judaea and reputedly buried here in a grave later forgotten, were rediscovered in the ninth century. A brilliant star directed Bishop Theodomir of Iria (otherwise Voghera) to the grave and ensured the saint an enormous following. The grave

became one of the most popular pilgrimages in all Christendom. A most astonishing ceremony, which takes place inside the building, is the swinging of *el botafumeiro*, a giant silver censer or thurible. Hauled by seven men on a rope fitted with pulleys, it zooms up to the roof and down again, with gusts of incense and spouting flames, while choirs sing and the organ thunders.

Below
Nazarenos – members of a *cofradía*, a brotherhood – on their way to take part in a procession in Jerez de la Frontera in Holy Week, 1983.

The greatest of such processions, fifty-two in all, take place in Seville.

Overleaf
Part of one of the enormous vineyards – altogether they amount to some 165,000 acres – where the golden Palomino grapes are grown from which sherry is made. Overlooking it is a *caserio*. Here the grapes are crushed underfoot by men who wear boots with long, protruding nails which squash the grapes but not the pips. The best vines are to be found in the *albarizas*, the areas in which chalk predominates. These vineyards shine with an almost unearthly light under the roasting sun.

Only here, in the sherry country between Cádiz and Seville, in the bars of Puerto de Santa Maria, Jerez de la Frontera and Sanlúcar de Barrameda, does a *copita* (a slender glass shaped like an upside-down funnel) of *fino*, the best and driest of sherries, taste as good. It is brought to you in a chilled half bottle, accompanied by little snacks called *tapas*.

Opposite
Participants in the great procession of Holy Week, Seville. Night and day during Holy Week, except for an hour or so after midday, the giant floats known as *pasos* are escorted through the streets. All of them are immensely heavy, embellished with silver, some decorated with flowers and bearing sumptuously dressed figures of the Virgin, and cost thousands of pounds each year to decorate (a Virgin's clothing and accessories alone have been valued at £100,000). The floats and figures are of inestimable worth,

some of the figures dating back to the sixteenth century: the oldest, the Cristo de Burgos, was carved in 1573. Some effigies depict events in the last six days of the life of Christ. All sway through the streets on the *pasos*, those carrying the Virgins like great ships illuminated by many, many candles, borne on the backs of sweating porters (some suffering deep wounds on their shoulders as a result), invisible beneath the velvet draperies.

From the deep canyons that are the streets of Seville, a city that is still partly Moorish, rise the fanfares of bugles and trumpets and the rolling of drums which accompany the playing of the marches peculiar to Holy Week. One such march, the *Armagura*, originally composed for the Crowned Virgin of Grief, *La Armagura Coronada*, is played so often that it might almost be regarded as the theme music of the *Semana Santa*.

Visions of a Battered Paradise

Turkey, 1966

THE first time I saw Istanbul was in 1956 when I finally arrived there in a Land Rover, seven days out from Barnes, SW13, after a shattering journey through the Balkans. As we drove along the last long stretch of road, lurching in the potholes, the Sea of Marmara appeared before us, green and windswept, deserted except for a solitary caique beating up towards the Bosphorus under a big press of sail. Our spirits rose at the thought of seeing Istanbul when the sun was setting, but when we reached the outskirts it was already dark. We had planned to enter the city by the Golden Gate on the seaward side, for it sounded romantic, not knowing that it had been sealed up for several hundred years. Instead we found ourselves on an interminable bypass lined with luminous advertisements for banks and razor blades. There was no sign of the land walls constructed by Theodosius in the first half of the fifth century, but they were still there.

Our next sight of Istanbul was almost exactly ten years later, in the spring of 1966. Again, we took seven days to drive from England, but they were less uncomfortable ones. This time we contrived to arrive in broad daylight.

> There is no lovelier scene on earth than that which opens up before the traveller as he approaches Constantinople from the Sea of Marmara . . . On the left, washed by the waves, the quaint old battlements extend from Seraglio Point to the Seven Towers, a distance of nearly four miles; and over them rise in picturesque confusion the terrace roofs, domes and minarets of Stamboul.

So wrote the anonymous author of the excellent *Handbook for Travellers* published by John Murray in 1878, which we happened to have with us.

The waters of Marmara no longer washed the battered walls of Byzantium. Below what remained of them, here on the seaward side, a wide corniche road ran along a barren and artificial foreshore, made up of rubble, to Seraglio Point, at the mouth of the Golden Horn, the inlet which divides the old city of Stamboul from the more modern, European quarter of Pera, or Beyoğlu to the north.

Here the road rounded Seraglio Point, off which unwanted odalisques were drowned in weighted sacks by the Palace gardeners (some sultans purged their harems of old stock in this manner with the regularity of careful motorists making an oil change). The greatest slaughter took place in the reign of the mad Sultan Ibrahim, who reigned from 1640 to 1649. He had 280 of his odalisques, the whole lot, drowned off Seraglio Point.

At the frontier near Edirne, in Thrace, we had provided ourselves with a copy of the Turkish Traffic Regulations in English, if only to see how many years it was possible to spend in prison by infringing them (a fate to be avoided at all costs). There were 'special speed limit for turcks and motorbikes', and 'unless

Rooftops of the Imperial Harem, Topkapi. A view of it that, until the deposition of Sultan Abd ul-Hamid II in 1909, few except the Sultan himself and his black eunuchs probably ever enjoyed, except when the members of the harem were at their summer quarters down by the Bosphorus near Seraglio Point. That year, the Young Turks who had deposed him caused circulars to be sent out to various parts of the Empire telling the parents of the odalisques – the women of the harem now unemployed – to come and reclaim them. 'The contrast,' Francis McCullagh wrote in his book, *The Fall of Abd ul-Hamid*, 'between the delicate complexions and costly attire of the women and the rough, weather-beaten appearance of the ill-clad mountaineers who had come to fetch them home was not the least striking feature of that extraordinary scene . . . The number of female slaves thus liberated was 216. Clad in Circassian peasant dress, they are now in all probability milking cows and doing farm work in Anatolia.'

diected by a sing or decree, it is forbidden to use the sounding devices unnecessarily or in a manner that would disturb public peace'.

No one, except ourselves, took the slightest notice of this edict, and if one was staying at an hotel it was necessary to insist on a room at least five floors up, and preferably facing away from the main road.

There were a million taxis, and what were known as 'dolmus' – which means 'stuffed' taxis. They followed fixed routes and were shared by a number of passengers, making them much cheaper than real taxis. However, if you were an obvious tourist, an empty, or unstuffed dolmus would instantly become a real taxi. But neither real nor stuffed taxis were, in fact, expensive.

In those days the driving was wild. Huge, beat-up American automobiles, which looked as if they had been hatched in the Prehistoric Department of the Natural History Museum, collided with one another, sometimes in threes and fours, and exploded in clouds of dust. When these had finally settled and expired, passengers emerged, apparently suffering from nothing worse than severe shock, and tottered away in search of yet another dolmus, as if realizing the futility of pursuing the matter at an official level.

Then there was a moment of glory when we crossed the Golden Horn by the floating Galata Bridge. On the far side of it was Galata, and above it on the hill, Pera. Ferry boats chugging to and from the Asian shore, belching black smoke, were packed together close up to the bridge at either end of it, which was heaving and groaning in the swell.

Out in the Bosphorus there were a couple of huge tankers on their way up in ballast to Batum, ships were at anchor in the entrance to the Golden Horn, scores of slender rowing boats danced on the water; and the air was filled with the whistling of ferry boats, the mooing of big ships' sirens, and the recorded cries of the muezzins from the minarets of a dozen or so mosques. It was also full of the kippery smell of fish being cooked, for the benefit of the passing trade, in open boats down by the approaches to the bridge, and – because the wind was blowing down the Golden Horn, from what was once the Sweet Waters of Europe, green arcadian meadows, the resort of ladies of the Imperial harem – the stench of tanneries was also in the air.

Looking back, a hazardous procedure when driving a Land Rover over the Galata Bridge, there was the incomparable skyline of Old Stamboul. To see Istanbul as it really should be seen, you had to climb a minaret. There were 240 steps choked with pigeon shit to the upper gallery of a minaret at the Sulemaniye mosque, and permission to make the climb was necessary from the head of the Muslim hierarchy, but it was worth it. Ahead was Pera with almost vertical cobbled streets leading up to the heights above. Pera exuded a melancholy rare even in the West; but now the preternaturally tall, nineteenth-century buildings, which made it so gloomy, are being torn down, and that is truly a loss to be bewailed.

On these slopes stood the Pera Palas Hotel. With the burning of Shepheard's in Cairo, the Pera Palas had become one of the few grand hotels to survive in the Near East. It had brass bedsteads and a suite once occupied by Atatürk, which looked as if it was being kept on regulo 1 for his return to earthly pleasures. Atatürk actually died in the Dolmabahçe Palace on 10 November 1938 at five past one, at which hour the innumerable clocks in the build-

The Galata Bridge on the Golden Horn, Istanbul, 1966.

When it is winter in Istanbul, and the wind comes off the Balkans or the Russian steppes (or wherever it does come from) laden with snow, it obliterates the city and makes mobility an even more hazardous business than when the sun is shining. In that now far-off winter, when this picture was taken, the two coldest sets of interiors I can remember were those of the Imperial Harem at Topkapi, and those (which finally finished us both off) of the twin Museums of the Ancient Orient and of Antiquities, in which innumerable wonders of the pre-classical and classical world were displayed in some forty enormous chambers. In such unbelievably cold conditions the best place to be was in one of those crazy wooden houses with stove pipes sticking out of them – these houses were always being burned down, if not being demolished – or in a hamam, otherwise a Turkish bath, of which there were reputed to be more than eighty. In fact, Istanbul in winter, or at any other time except high summer, is my favourite city.

ing were all stopped for ever.

High above it, hidden in the woods, was Yildiz, the palace built by Sultan Abd ul-Hamid II, one of the loneliest men in Europe. Here he constructed a labyrinth of tunnels in which he could take refuge from assassins, and keep up his pistol practice, taking coffee with himself in a number of kiosks which he erected for this purpose.

On the far, Asian shore were the Sweet Waters of Asia, more waterside meadows where the Sultan and his court spent their summer leisure days. Less despoiled than the Sweet Waters of Europe, it was now a fairground. All along this Asian shore the beautiful wooden *yalis*, the

Above

A street on the old Stamboul side of the Golden Horn, beyond the Atatürk Bridge, a part of the city few tourists ever see. Here, in the district called Fener, the Greeks lived until comparatively recently. The Jewish quarter was in Balat, next door to it. Some of these Jews were Greek speaking and their ancestors had lived in the city from the time when it was still Byzantium. Others, members of the Sephardim, had emigrated to Constantinople from Spain in 1492, and some of these still continued to speak the medieval Ladino, and may still do so to this day.

Of all the eccentric constructions in Istanbul, the demountable church of St Stephen of the Bulgars at Balat is probably the most remarkable. A church made of cast iron, it was shipped in sections from Vienna in 1871 on one hundred barges, travelling down the Danube, through the Black Sea and the Bosphorus, and was finally put together with nuts and bolts on the shores of the Golden Horn.

Opposite

A *hamal* (porter) carrying an immense load of canvas up to one of the *hans* (caravanserais) on the periphery of the Great Covered Bazaar, the Kapali Çarşisi, in Istanbul.

houses that in some cases overhung the water, were now so ruinous that they were actually falling into it. Out in the stream, the water, which was still reasonably unpolluted, was green and very cold and seethed like water in a boiling pot. Jellyfish abounded.

The enormous Selimiye Barracks were also on the Asian shore of the Bosphorus, facing the entrance to the Golden Horn in Üsküdar. It was here that Florence Nightingale tended the Crimean wounded – the cemetery in which those who died were buried was close by. Üsküdar was a place of mosques and cemeteries. Nearby was the largest Muslim cemetery in Asia. Hordes of the faithful were laid to rest among the cypress trees, together with the saintly Karaca Ahmet and his favourite horse.

The Kapali Çarşisi, the Great Bazaar, was a city hidden within a city. It had 18 doors all locked at night and guarded by savage dogs, 66 named streets, five mosques, countless cupolas, and covered an area of 47 acres – 51.7 if one included a number of the neighbouring *hans* (caravanserais). Yet it was still possible to find oases of calm in its long passages, such as those in the northern part rarely visited by tourists because the shops only sold skins, plastic foam and other items which not even the most demented tourist would have wanted to cart away.

The *hans* were built round open courts in which the animals of the caravans were once tethered. Leading off the vaulted corridors on the upper storeys were the rooms which provided accommodation for the merchants and their drivers. Some were now occupied by metal workers, but they still had an exciting aspect, especially at night when they were illuminated by fires and furnaces. These and the underground cisterns of the city of which more

than eighty had been discovered were among the most extraordinary remains in Istanbul.

In the cistern known as Yerebatan Saray, 'The Buried Palace', twelve rows of 28 reddish brown columns – with mottled green stains on some of them – topped by Byzantine Corinthian capitals, rose from the water like the boles of enormous trees in a flooded forest. The columns, carved with the marks of the men who erected them in the sixth century, in the time of Justinian, soared up into the murk towards the invisible roof. Half of their height was embedded in the silt beneath our feet. Another was the Binbirdirek, 'The Thousand and One Columns', a slight oriental hyperbole, since there were only 224 originally, but it was no less impressive for that. Built possibly by a Roman senator in the sixth century in the time of Constantine the Great, it was entered through a decrepit building in a quiet square, in which the custodian switched on the illuminations by hooking a couple of bare wires to the main, and you descended a flight of steps through what resembled, in winter, a thick fog. In this cistern the only water was that which dripped from the roof.

Above ground, close by, behind Haghia Sophia, and inside the Imperial gate of the Seraglio (Top Kapi), was the basilica of Haghia Eirene (the Divine Peace); a vast, empty building with ochre walls, a dark cross in mosaic on the vault of the apse, and below it the patriarch's throne with six tiers of seats in a semicircle for the clergy. Outside this church, in the year 346, three thousand people were killed in a confrontation between two bands of Christians: the Arians and the orthodox upholders of the Nicene Creed.

This church was one of the most memorable Christian buildings in Istanbul. The Kariye Camii, otherwise St Saviour in Chora, out by the northwestern walls through which the Turks broke into the city in 1453, was another. This little sixth-century church, which later became a mosque, had singularly beautiful mosaics and wall paintings which were brought to light and restored in 1958.

And there was the palace of Topkapi. At that time the Harem had not yet been opened to the public, but by pulling a number of strings we were admitted to a part of it – a bitterly cold 400-room labyrinth on several floors, room after echoing room, abandoned and scarcely ever opened since Abd ul-Medjid I, the last Sultan to maintain a harem there, left it in 1853 to live in the Dolmabahçe Palace. Most macabre were the quarters occupied by the Black Eunuchs on duty, the Karagalar Tasligi, three storeys high, more like a deep ditch than a human habitation, its only ornament a great gaping fireplace on the ground floor, now full of fallen rubble. In the reign of Murad III (1574–95) there were between six and eight hundred Black Eunuchs who had entry to the Harem, most of whom must have lived outside. Murad III had 1200 harem women, by whom he had 103 children. Twenty sons and twenty-seven daughters survived him. His eldest son, who succeeded him as Mehmet III, had all his nineteen brothers put to death and seven of his father's pregnant concubines drowned.

The only sounds in this strange place were those made by the hordes of bats, mice behind the wainscotings, and the whistling of the ferry boats in the Bosphorus.

Below
Shepherd and flock in the necropolis of ancient Hierapolis, now Pamukkale.

Overleaf

A spectator (long since removed to a museum) in the great theatre at Side – one of the largest theatres in Asia Minor – which could seat twenty thousand people, here seen in its still pristine state of ruin in 1965. It stands on a peninsula, and, although the whole area has been subjected to extensive development, in other words mucked about, there are still remarkable views to be had from the top of it.

A lion up a tree, Lake Manyara National Park, 1971.

No one really knows why some African lions in a few places climb trees. One other such lion is, or was, at Ishasha, in the Queen Elizabeth Park in Uganda, probably attempting to get away from tsetse flies, or perhaps from Idi Amin – no friend to wild life. Some say that lions climb trees to avoid getting tummy chills from lying on swampy ground (there are large areas of ground-water forest with giant fig and mahogany trees growing in them in the Manyara Park); others, that it is to enable them to see over tall grass, or simply because it is cooler thirty feet or so up in the air. Certainly it is not so that they can jump on to the roofs of the buses in order to be nearer the tourists.

Treetops

East Africa, 1967

WHEN I went to East Africa for the first time in 1967 I took with me *Hints to Travellers*, published by the Royal Geographical Society in 1937, which was full of useful information, such as:

In the Ruwenzori it was customary to give the porters a Cerebos salt tin full of *bulo* flour, besides salt and blankets. This corresponds to a native measure, a *kiraba*. Loads are made up to 45 lbs, rather less than the weights of loads carried on safari in the plains . . . Cutters who make a way in advance of the porters often go off at right angles to the direction indicated, either because the path is easier or for some reason known only to themselves.

Things had changed a bit in Africa since this was written. No one walked more than a few feet on the modern, motorized, packaged safaris; no African carried a minimal 45 lbs of your belongings on his noddle; no one gave anyone a *kiraba* of *bulo* any more; and instead of employing wood cutters to clear a way to the extraordinary Ruwenzori mountains you could contemplate them from the neighbourhood of the Mountains of the Moon Hotel at Fort Portal in Uganda – telegram address 'Romance'. 'Cracking log fires. Nine-hole golf course. Pygmy village. Hot springs in which an egg is perfectly boiled by nature.' (Did you whisper 'four minutes please' as you dropped it in and hope for a piece of African magic?)

It is one's first encounter with wild animals, other than animals in cages, that really sticks in the mind, however banal the circumstances. In my case, in Africa, my first exposure to them took place after Sunday curry at the Outspan Hotel at Nyeri, a morning's drive north of Nairobi in the lands of the, until fairly recently, not all that friendly Kikuyu tribe. We piled into Land Rovers – not really necessary for such a trip but they gave an atmosphere – and set off for Treetops, the lodge at the foot of the Aberdare Range. After crossing a six-foot-deep ditch dug to keep the elephant out of the surrounding farm land, we walked the few hundred yards to the lodge, accompanied by an ex-Indian Army colonel, armed with a rifle. There was a strong feral smell in the air.

'Keep together,' he said. 'There are elephant about.' The Japanese in the party, who were loaded with a multiplicity of cameras and lenses, had what was surely a dangerous tendency to lag behind and point 500-mm lenses at little flowers. Sure enough, there on the track were four large dollops of what looked like Old Auntie Mary's rich Dundee cake still steaming from the oven, the new-laid droppings of an elephant. Everyone was impressed and one of the Japanese photographed them in colour. The rest of us scuttled after the colonel.

The new Treetops, unlike the old one in which Princess Elizabeth became Queen and which was burned down in the time of the Mau Mau, was not really in a tree at all, although branches writhed unexpectedly in the corridors. It stood

on piles above a large pool and salt lick, the edge of which was so trodden by animals that from the upper floors of the lodge it looked like an aerial view of Passchendaele.

Treetops was all right. Had it not been to our liking it would have been just too bad, because we were locked up in it until the next morning.

On the far side of the pool, warthogs and their young were zooming round in circles; a huge, rare, black, giant forest hog was looking at a battered tree as if deciding whether to demolish it or not; and up on the sun deck of the lodge there were baboons, with inflamed faces and even more alarming effects at their other ends, careering about, knocking over loaded Pentaxes, pinching the sandwiches laid out for afternoon tea, and disappearing rudely between ladies' legs. In addition, black-headed orioles in the Cape chestnut trees made fruity noises, and thousands of weaver birds were seething away in a bed of reeds in the middle of the pool. The noise was terrible. We were told to keep quiet so as not to frighten the animals. It seemed a superfluous warning, like telling children at a cocktail party to pipe down.

But that was nothing to the bedlam which broke loose when night fell, and the baboons and their young had departed, and the weaver birds had taken to their swinging nests in the reeds. There had been rain in the bamboo forests high in the Aberdares, and to escape it the animals had come down in force. At any one time throughout the night there were fifty elephant outside the lodge under the floodlights, all taking up trunk-loads of mud packed with health-giving mineral salts; black buffalo wallowed in it so deep that only the huge black handlebars that were their horns showed; rhinos wallowed less deeply – all were the uniform saffron colour of the mud. All species, including the various sorts of buck, observed a wary apartheid. As in the world of men there was a lot of confrontation and a lot of backing down – everything feared the buffalo. Only the rhino really faced up to one another, and when one of them slipped his opponent a length of allegedly aphrodisiac horn, it went lumbering off into the forest, groaning.

It is the noises they all made that I remember: gaseous noises; sounds like heavy furniture which has lost its castors being moved across a room; the sounds of the last water going down the plug hole; even more weird gurglings and the sound you produce when you blow into a funnel.

Treetops was perhaps the one hotel in the world where, if you could only get to sleep, you could share a double room (you had to whether you liked it or not) and snore to your heart's content; but sleep by night was impossible and a waste of valuable viewing time. When the swift African dawn came around six thirty, the animals were still there, stuck in the mud, and I was hooked on East Africa.

A solitary zebra in the Ngorongoro Crater.

To the west of the Crater Conservation Area, which covered 2500 square miles, was the Serengeti National Park, also in Tanzania, 5700 square miles of it, most of it vast open plains, between 3000 and 5000 feet above the sea. Giant migrations of zebra and wildebeest took place here in May and June westwards from the plains into the narrow corridor which extends to within a few miles of Lake Victoria. On these migrations they were attended by various carnivora which preyed on them, including the terrible wild dog. The west–east migration took place in November–December.

Below

Masai tribesman, Ngorongoro Crater, Tanzania, 1968.

At sunrise I was standing on the rim of the crater which is nine miles across, between 2000 and 2500 feet deep, and covers 100 square miles, when suddenly two young Masai appeared from over the edge. The crater was full of mist, and the sun was shining on it. Everything, including the two Masai, was an unearthly shade of red. Even I could see that one of the great photographs of all time was there for the taking. With me was Ian Berry, the famous Magnum photographer, who was armed with a number of Leicas. After he had shot the Masai, and they had gone on their way, he discovered that what he had in his cameras was not high-speed Ektachrome but Kodachrome II (which has an immutable processing technique), and his ASA ratings were all wrong. He was so upset that he wouldn't speak for days, and my humble black-and-white shot is the only record of this melancholy happening.

Opposite

Muso-o-Tunya – The Smoke That Thunders. Otherwise the Victoria Falls, from the Zambian side of the Zambezi, 1971. To me it looked more like molten metal than water, as it slid rather than ran gently downhill through an archipelago of boulders to the edge of a trench, a mile long and twice as deep as Niagara, sliced through the basalt of the African plateau. There, it seemed to hesitate before dropping into the rift, which looked like a one-way trip to eternity, and the great clouds of vapour that resulted – as high again as the Falls themselves – could be seen up to twenty miles away.

The Zambians were said to be touchy (their leaders certainly were) about Livingstone and his claim to have 'discovered' the Falls in 1855, on the edge of which their ancestors had been camping out for goodness knows how long before that. So much for the unfortunate Livingstone, and about 90 per cent of all other explorers, who, by the same reasoning, are reduced to the status of non-starters in the discovery stakes.

Where Europe Ends

Portugal, 1969

A T 9.30 a.m. on All Saints' Day, Saturday, 1 November 1755, the great Lisbon earthquake began. Within ten minutes there were three major shocks accompanied by awful, apocalyptical rumblings. The towers and spires of the churches, which were filled with worshippers, swayed and toppled and the buildings collapsed on the congregations.

Dust turned day into night; fires broke out; and the Tagus rose over its banks in three huge waves, inundating the lower part of the city. The palaces of the rich, the hovels of the poor, convents, libraries, art collections, the immense treasure looted from Africa, India and Brazil; even, to the delight of the majority, the headquarters of the Inquisition which had sentenced the indigenous inhabitants of Goa and other overseas dominions to be burned alive at the auto-da-fé wearing yellow dunces' caps with the same enthusiasm as they had committed their fellow countrymen to the flames, collapsed. The entire centre of the city and an estimated ten thousand buildings of what one Spanish writer described as 'this eighth wonder, the greatest in Christendom, this outstanding city, famous and noble', were largely consumed. Out of a population of about 275,000, more than 30,000 lost their lives.

The earthquake marked the end of an era. The British and Hamburg merchants never again enjoyed the same influence in the city. After it the belief in divine and benevolent providence was rudely attacked by Voltaire and *Candide* became a best-seller. The optimism of Pope and Rousseau and the pre-established harmony of Leibnitz no longer sounded so good in Lisbon anymore, or anywhere else.

But the city recovered. In twenty years it rose splendidly from its ashes under the able direction of the Marquês de Pombal, Minister of José I, an absolute dictator of a sort which the Portuguese seem to stand in need of and positively relish at times.

Lisbon was a very soberly dressed city. Bourgeois ambition was a beaded dress for dinner with your husband and his boss and his wife and a Persian lamb coat with a mink collar for winter. The reason why so many ladies in Lisbon smelt of mothballs, even if they never owned a fur coat, was because mothballs were supposed to ward off bad luck. They certainly warded off me. Their menfolk appeared to wear subfusc suits and white shirts at all times, except when on a beach or in bed.

Even though the Baixa (pronounced Baïcha, if that is any help) or Lower Town is an elegant shopping area you soon began to realize that this was, for all the outward show, the desperately poor capital of a desperately poor country. Many people lived on the outskirts in what were nothing more than brick huts with no water supply. You could see such townships of hovels in the Alcântara Valley where the great aqueduct, the Aqueducto das Águas Livres, crossed it.

You realized it, too, because in this city there were almost more sellers of lottery tickets than potential buyers.

Lisbon. Part of the Baixa (the Lower Town) seen from the *Elevador*, the passenger lift built by Eiffel (of the Tower) which links it with the Largo do Carmo in the upper part.

Not only men and women without arms, legs and eyes, but others, unmutilated, some of whom looked as if they might once have been bank managers who had had their banks fold under them.

And there were lots of beggars whom the Lisboans, a kindly lot on the whole, had the pleasant habit of rewarding rather than ignoring.

As evening fell, you could see whole families of what were known as *Ferro Velho*, otherwise the *Homens do Papétar*, the Men of the Paper, women and children included, scavenging the cardboard and paper from outside shops and offices and lugging it away to sell it to middle men in the scrap paper business. Nothing was wasted by the poor of this city. Anything that was broken here could and would be repaired. They did not understand the meaning of 'replace the unit', which was why, added to the strange cries uttered by the *varinhas*, the fishwives and those of the innumerable sellers of roast chestnuts whose smoking stoves each winter plunged the streets into a species of fog, you could hear the equally weird sound of the Pan pipes played by the Galician repairers of umbrellas who wheeled their bikes around the streets loaded with old ones which they cannibalized for the ribs. Galician knifegrinders also played the same instruments to attract customers.

But if you think that because of all this scarcely concealed poverty the shopkeepers and the assistants in any of the more expensive shopping streets were going to encourage you to acquire anything on their premises, you have another think coming. While down in the fish and fruit and veg. markets women were positively pressing one to pick up 20 metres or so of conger eel, a sack or two of potatoes or half a dozen pineapples, wherever the shops had plate glass windows you were going to encounter something peculiarly Portuguese, which is the sales person's resistance to selling anything. To attempt to buy in a department store one of the hideous pottery roosters that come from Barcelos in northwest Portugal was like trying to shop in a family vault.

Out to the west, above the Tagus, in Mandragoa, was where the *varinhas* lived, together with their families. They came originally from Ovar, a fishing town on the lagoons south of Oporto, and most of them lived in a labyrinth of dwellings that was once a convent. It was they who bought the freshly landed catches down on the waterfront and then trotted off through the streets with the fish on their heads in wicker baskets, crying in their impossible dialect the equivalent of 'Fresh mackerel', 'Fresh sardines', or whatever fish they had to offer.

Dark-skinned, some of them young and saucy, others more severe, some pear-shaped with legs like boles of trees, they looked as if they would be capable of supporting the whole world on their heads in addition to a hundred pounds or so weight of fish. They wore black shawls, short, bunchy black skirts, aprons, gold hoops in their ears and round their necks gold necklaces with hearts and crosses hanging from them.

Now, in the 1980s, their numbers have been reinforced by a whole host of brightly dressed negresses who, together with their husbands, have migrated here from the Cape Verde Islands, and when they are seen as an ensemble with the black-clad *varinhas*, down on the waterfront, they look like the chorus line of some fishy musical about to burst into dance and song.

On either side of the valley in which Pombal's city stands were the old quarters: the Alfama, built in the sixteenth century, and to the west the Bairro Alto, which had been seriously affected by tourists, reached by way of the Elevador, a fantastic lift designed by Eiffel of the Tower. The Alfama was also much frequented by tourists but strangely unaffected by them; the Bairro Alto, a criss-cross of narrow streets as deep as canyons, some with exciting, unexpected views of the Tagus, was by day full of artisans in little workshops turning out objects that were only a memory in most other Western countries. Here, some of the restaurants were so small that six customers made a quorum and even then the fish had to be grilled outside on the pavement.

In the afternoon the tarts began to appear on the street corners. Some looked more like maiden aunts than tarts. At night the Bairro Alto finally woke up, and the *fado* could be heard. But to hear the *fado* sung properly it was necessary to cross the valley to Alfama. *Fado* is sung by ladies of a certain age; ripe would not be an uncomplimentary description. And they are always dressed in black. It is tremulous, and infinitely melancholic, and its origins are disreputable.

In Lisbon, as indeed almost anywhere else, it is to the Alfama and similar quarters that one returns. Those in which the manifest happiness of the furless, tieless inhabitants appears to be in inverse proportion to their wealth. In the narrow streets into which cars seldom penetrated, in which the washing billowed out like well-drawing spinnakers; streets in which there were odd smells, not all of them unpleasant, not all of them agreeable, but streets, something becoming increasingly rare in the modern world, in which you were not made to feel unwelcome.

*   *   *

The country around Lisbon and to the immediate north of it is very different to that of the Alentejo, and the Algarve in the south, which in the late 1960s was only just beginning to be developed. Much of it was lush and green, and further north of Lisbon, in the Beira Litoral, there were enormous pine forests, first planted in the thirteenth century.

But it was the number of large, old buildings which made this country different from the south. Down in the Alentejo, beyond the endless main road, there seemed to be no other roads at all, no other villages among the red earth. There I felt that a properly mounted expedition would be needed to penetrate those fastnesses among the eerie cork trees, in which only an occasional white farmhouse loomed on a hill. Down there it was comparatively rare to see a monastery or even a large secular building, apart from the farmhouses.

The north, on the other hand, was full of palaces, convents, monasteries and churches, many of them built in splendid isolation and on such a heroic scale it seemed impossible that they could ever have had their full complement of the courtiers, nuns, monks or congregations they were designed to house. Now for the most part they were uninhabited, except by hordes of custodians. Visiting them it was necessary to be equipped with plenty of small change – they both needed and appreciated it.

Among the most extraordinary of these large buildings was the Ajuda Palace above Belém, from which da Gama's little fleet set sail for India in 1497, returning in 1499. Begun in 1816, but never finished (its last occupant was the Queen Dowager Maria Pia, who died in 1911), it was permeated with that unique form of Portuguese melancholy known as the *saudade* and housed one of the world's great collections of uncomfortable furniture – a whole set of porcelain furniture was a gift from the King of Saxony. There was also a collection of awful paintings, some of them very funny. Long corridors, in which a perpetual twilight reigned, were lined with glass cases stuffed with unwanted wedding presents, some of really hideous ingenuity.

Somewhat different was the Queluz Palace, which was pink and very pretty, built in 1758 for Prince Pedro, who married his niece. Even nicer were the gardens with their box hedges, mazes, cages for wild beasts (now empty), statues – some very strange (sphinx heads with ruffs round their necks) – and the Dutch Canal, its walls lined with blue and white glazed tiles with marine scenes painted on them. And beyond that there was Sintra, in the Serra de Sintra, only 17 miles from Lisbon. It is difficult to exaggerate the romantic beauty of Sintra and the mountains in which it lay concealed, with great trees growing out of an almost endless chaos of rocks, which, wreathed in mist as they so often were, seemed like the work of an artist of the Sung dynasty. In the environs of the little town itself, the dark lanes with their moss-grown walls, and the sudden, surprising views of palaces and huge houses raising their extraordinary spires, towers and grotesque chimneys among the trees, created a powerful impression but not one that was altogether agreeable.

One of these great follies was the Pena Palace, built in the mid-nineteenth century as a summer residence for Ferdinand of Saxe-Coburg-Gotha, a cousin of Prince Albert and consort of Maria II. It, too, was permeated with the *saudade*, and also an overwhelming smell of furniture polish which the state apparently dispensed to the custodians by the ton. The official policy with regard to an ancient building in Portugal at that time was, 'If you can't get permission to knock it down, make it like new and polish it.' The Portuguese were great knockers-down of old buildings at that time, often doing so in the pursuit of what they called *urbanização*, urbanization.

Seven miles from the town, hidden away among even bigger, mossier rocks than one had so far seen, was the Convento de Capuchos, abandoned by the monks in the last century, its gloomy cells entirely walled and furnished with cork. William Beckford, who visited the convent in 1797, described it with the Capuchin monks at table, eating great mounds of greasy food, and presided over by their drunken Father Guardian, exactly as it might have been in a painting by Magnasco.

At São Pedro de Sintra, highest of the three Sintras (the other two were Sintra and Santa Maria), on the second and fourth Sundays of each month a remarkable market was held in its triangular square, one of the last such markets to be held close to the capital.

At that time there were still, in spite of the preponderance of plastic objects, a lot of genuine country artefacts on sale, as well as some interesting, semi-antique junk. Here, too, in the upper part of this square, in the Cantinho de S. Pedro, you could drink a delicious white wine from barrels, in the company of shepherds and farmers.

North of Sintra the road to Mafra ran through open, rather lonely country, now much changed, at that time full of windmills which were still functioning. The sails of these windmills were of canvas and could be furled in the same way as a sail, and attached to them on ropes there

Opposite
A non-market day in the triangular marketplace in São Pedro de Sintra, still one of the more authentic markets near Lisbon, but one which only takes place on the second and fourth Sunday of each month.

Overleaf
Windmills fitted with canvas sails and terracotta whistles, still functioning in the 1960s in what was then the lonely country between Sintra and Mafra. Now it has been built over and is very industrialized.

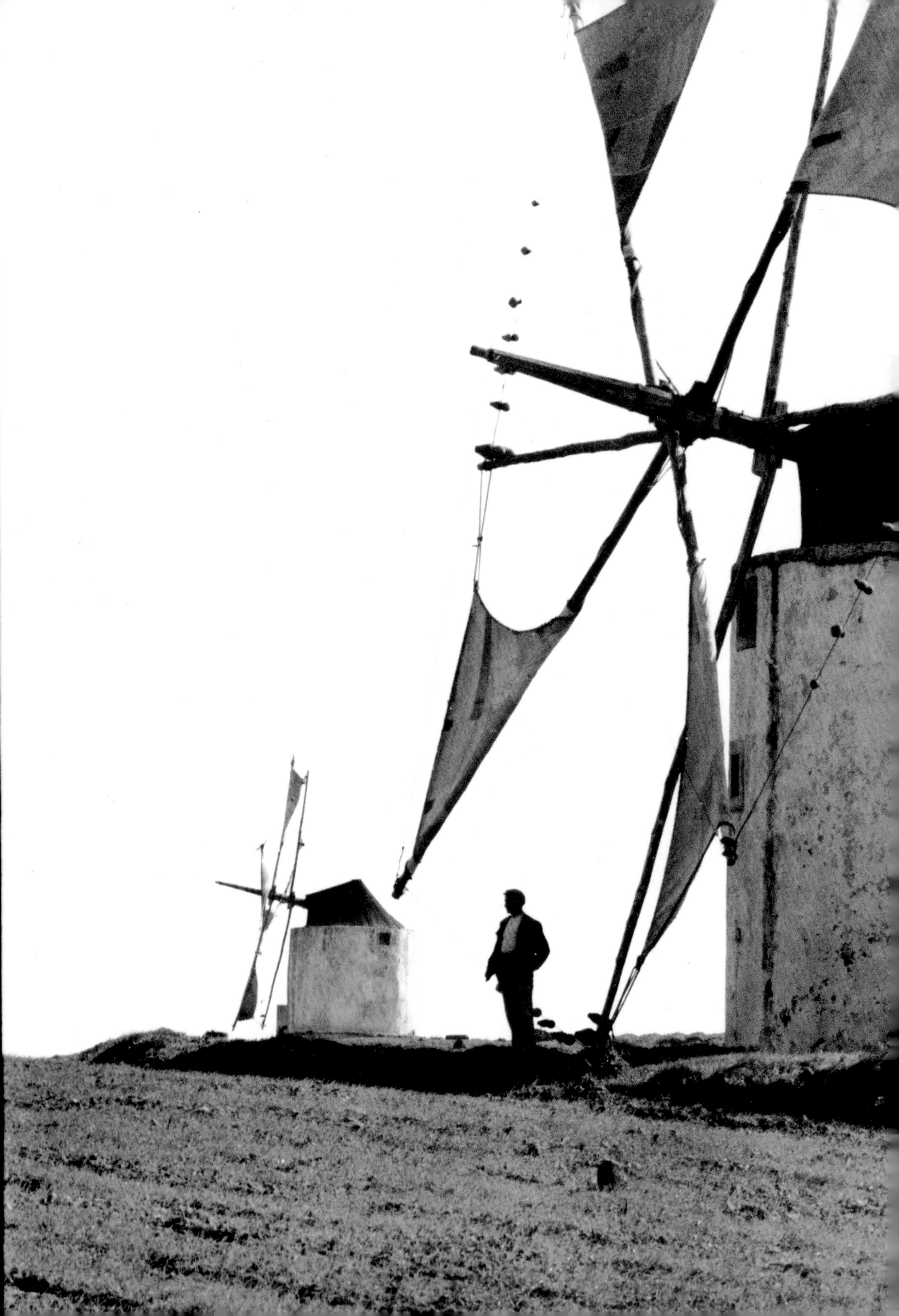

were clay whistles which when they rotated and the wind blew through them produced eerie sounds.

It is doubtful if even the Portuguese in the interest of *urbanização* will ever summon up the resolution to demolish the Convent of Mafra which is bigger than the Escorial. Designed by a German architect to the order of King John V in 1717, it took thirteen years to build. By 1730, 45,000 were employed in its construction. The cost of it helped Portugal on her way to financial ruin. Although it contained little that was memorable apart from a beautiful rococo library – there was a particularly lugubrious room entirely furnished with furniture constructed from the skins and antlers of stags – it did have an undeniably nightmarish quality about it, principally because of its ability to reduce everyone within its walls to the stature of pygmies.

Further north was Obidos, a beautiful but over-restored walled town, a sort of Portuguese Clovelly. Even in the off-season when we were there and they were not engaged in selling objects to tourists, the inhabitants of Obidos were so muted that one wondered if they, too, had been given the restoration treatment.

North of it, on the coast, was Nazaré, a strange fishing village with even stranger inhabitants, situated in the shadow of a sheer cliff. Here, an entire community lived out its life for all to see, women, children and the aged on shore, the younger, more active men out on the sea fishing, all in costume. The women wore full skirts in big check patterns, inflated by layer upon layer of petticoats, black, fringed shawls and golden earrings. The men wore checked trousers and shirts.

The bringing in of the brightly painted boats to the beach and the hauling out of the boats with the help of oxen was a ritual. Now, in 1969, was it done for the tourists, or for their own, private delectation? Would they have preferred to use tractors instead of oxen? we wondered. None of those we asked could or would say. It was a mystery. Not that they lacked for words: 'Gimme cigarette!' the men said in English in all the bars, these picturesque-looking men in their checks. 'You give me one!' I said, fed up with their pestering ways – and sometimes they did.

North of Nazaré and about forty miles south of Oporto, was Aveiro, on the landward side of an extensive labyrinth of lagoons, a town penetrated by canals spanned by humped-backed bridges. It was a place of mirages. In the distance, across the salt pans, some of the big three- and four-masted schooners of Portugal's cod-fishing fleet loomed up in an unearthly haze. The fleet spent eight months of the year at sea, much of it on the Grand Banks or in the Davis Strait, as ships of the Portuguese fishing fleet had always done ever since the sixteenth century. (Now, since the end of the sixties, this staple food of Catholic countries comes from Scandinavia and the Portuguese fleet is no more.)

Beyond this place where the ships were laid up, a road lined with tamarisk wriggled through the sands which separated the lagoon from the Atlantic, to Barra, a village dominated by an enormous lighthouse which rose up at the end of the main street. Beyond that was Costa Nova do Prado with a church standing alone on the sands on which the surf thundered incessantly.

Opposite
Part of Portugal's fleet of cod-fishing schooners, laid up in one of the lagoons at Aveiro, south of Oporto, a fleet that is now no more. The little shops on this Atlantic coast, and all the way up it to Galicia, were more or less carbon copies of their counterparts on the west coast of Ireland – full of gum boots.

Overleaf
The beach at Nazaré.

Opposite
A lagoon at Aveiro. Once unique in its feeling of isolation, its shores are now lined with holiday homes.

Above
Costa Nova do Prado. Here the only sounds were the flapping of the washing and the boom of the Atlantic surf on the dunes. A place where I felt I could have stayed for ever. It, too, has been given the holiday-homes treatment.

Morning of the World
Bali, 1969

ROHIBITED from Entry', warned the Indonesian Customs Excise Declarations which we filled in on the plane, 'Weapons, narcotics, phornography (without special licence)'. They needn't have worried. This was one of the places where no one needed phornography, with or without a licence.

When Nehru visited Bali in 1954 he described it as being a place which was like the 'Morning of the World', and going there fifteen years later I wondered if this was the sort of oriental hyperbole which statesmen utter when leaving countries in which they have been lavishly entertained, but in this case he was absolutely right. Even before we arrived, flying over Java and looking down into the enormous, reeking maws of 10,000-foot-high volcanoes, one of them hiding a bright blue lake within, we were sure that we were on our way to something extraordinary.

The island itself was beautiful but no more entrancing than many other places in the East. There were other wild shores, equally or even more lovely, on the coasts of Malabar or Coromandel; there were no great, lost cities, buried for centuries in the jungle, such as Angkor Wat or Gaur in southern India, and even the biggest temple – the Balinese are Hindus – was not as stupefyingly large as Borobodur, across the narrow straits in Java, or as extravagant as Konorak, hidden away in the sands on the shore of the Bay of Bengal.

But, even if the temples were not all that big, there were said to be ten thousand in Bali and there may have been many more, for every house had a Hindu shrine and many of them were large enough to qualify as temples, and Bali is about twenty times the size of the Isle of Wight and much the same shape. They seemed much less frequented than those in India, the little doors of the tabernacles were mostly shut in the day time, and less creepy. Here, as well as in the temples, offerings were made in the dust of the road, on the floor of a shop, in the narrowest part of a bazaar, a rectangle of plaited palm leaf with marigolds and other flowers on it. Even a great cave in the interior, with a monster carved over the entrance who seemed to be splitting the rock in two with his demoniacal strength, had none of the eerie dottiness of the caves in *A Passage to India*, no bats, only a passive statue of the elephant god, Ganesh, in a niche, waiting for someone to illuminate him momentarily with a gas lighter. In Bali I had none of the batty theological conversations I used to have in India, principally because I couldn't speak the language.

It was the human beings that were so extraordinary in Bali, so small, so finely made. To them a European five foot nine tall must have resembled Goliath. All their lives the women here carried immense weights on their heads and in order to do so they had to stand very upright. This gave them immense grace even when they were carrying nothing but themselves.

In Denpasar, the capital, which at

that time had few if any buildings more than three storeys high, the builders' mates were all women who scaled vertical ladders amongst forests of wooden scaffolding carrying sixty or seventy pounds of masonry on their lovely little noddles. In Denpasar, too, there were congeries of markets, entirely staffed by women, hundreds of them. One of these markets, down by the bridge over the river which bisected the main street, hidden away, huge and dark green, with long shafts of light shining down into it, so that it looked like a city sunk beneath the sea, dealt in spices and three-year-old eggs wrapped in mud. Another sold temple furnishings, exquisite objects made from cane, magnificently painted baskets and beautiful door knobs. On the other side of the river, in the fruit market, the owners of fighting cocks squatted, cosseting them before the next bloodthirsty meeting that would make bankrupts of some of their owners, while girls trotted by carrying long baskets full of suckling pigs which when roasted became a delicious dish called *babi guling*.

There were far fewer breasts exposed on Bali than there had been before the war. It was no longer *'L'Isle des Seins Nus'*. Two and a half years of Japanese military occupation and the endless pointing at them of Nikons and Pentaxes had caused a subsequent withdrawal from general view of these beautiful objects but they could still be seen, fleetingly displayed, at bathing places by rivers, in gardens, and were of course always at hand for thirsty infants.

You would have had to have had a heart of stone to ignore the people of this island, or have been stone deaf, for this was a place of constant greeting, so that you were constrained to memorize at least one or two greet-

ings and farewells in the language to use along the way. However, employing them ourselves, we did not always get the enthusiastic response we expected. This was because the universal greeting between visitors and visited was 'Ullo!', to which the only possible reply was 'Ullo!' No other greeting or response gave such unanimous pleasure.

Here we were 'Ulloed!' by delicious girls whose Western counterparts would have given me an icy stare if I had 'Ulloed!' them up the junction, by small boys up in the rigging of fruit trees, by men at the bottom of wells they were digging and by cohorts of pot-bellied infants standing in doorways.

Out in the country the Balinese, who were among the most skilful rice growers in the East, had created a wonderful, artificial world of terraced rice fields which followed the contours of the hills and valleys, so that looking at them was as if one was looking at the layered contours of a sophisticated map. The distribution of water to the rice fields, which were filled with ducks, from the rivers which burrowed down from the mountains, sometimes a hundred feet below ground level, was a complicated business. Water was carried across gorges in bamboo pipes, and along irrigation ditches on the steep sides of valleys. Sometimes it vanished into the sides of hills.

This distribution, and every other sort of village activity, agricultural, social and religious, was controlled by the *Bandjar*, a sort of voluntary village government. It had been so successful that the government was introducing the system to other parts of Indonesia.

The *Bandjar* also owned the tilling equipment, the meeting halls, the instruments belonging to the village orchestras and the dance costumes, some of which were extremely valu-

able. It was possible to attend a village dance every night of one's stay in Bali and some people did nothing else.

All the activities of the *Bandjar* were accompanied by religious observances. Scarcely any action took place without some sort of esoteric sanction, whether it was the planting of rice, the filing of teeth, the painting of pictures, or the cremation of the dead.

Waiting in a funeral house for the procession to the cremation place to begin.

To the Balinese the cremation of the dead is the most sacred and necessary duty that they are called upon to perform. It is an event so costly that the bodies of less well-off individuals have to be interred in sand, sometimes for years, before enough money can be accumulated by the relatives to bear the cost of the animated, cheerful and beautiful cremation ceremonies.

The day before the ceremony, the effigies of the dead were taken to the house of the priest to be blessed, and there was dancing and the performance of a shadow play, something at which the Balinese are very adept.

Before the cremation the actual remains were watched over by relatives of the deceased who came from far and near. On the day of the cremation the great, tall, extravagantly decorated cremation towers were loaded with these remains and carried to the burning ground, together with a number of sarcophagi made in the form of bulls and cows. They were accompanied by a long procession of women, carrying offerings on their heads, dancers and an orchestra which played Balinese music which, with its strange percussive effects, resembles bursts of machine-gun fire. Can this be why it is so endearing to Western ears?

The towers, carried by twenty or thirty men, reeled and gyrated as the bearers purposely tried to make the dead lose their sense of direction so that they could never find their way back to the houses from which they came.

Next, chickens were released from the towers and the remains of the dead were transferred to the interiors of the bull and cow sarcophagi which were then filled with offerings by the relatives through a hole slit in the top. Then everything went up in fire and smoke, lit by burning glasses in the afternoon sun.

The following day a great procession escorted the ashes to the sea where they were scattered on the water and the whole host of people bathed in order to purify themselves. This was one of the most exciting and joyous spectacles left to us on earth, not a whiff of formaldehyde. Here, the whole width of the Pacific Ocean separated us from Whispering Glades.

These scenes made it all the more difficult to believe that at least 50,000 Hindu Balinese with communist sympathies had been killed there during the winter of 1965/66 by the Indonesian army with the help of the Indonesian Muslims. Altogether, during this period, the number of Communists killed has been estimated at between 100,000 and a million – the biggest defeat the movement has so far suffered in its history.

Way Down the Wakwayowkastic River

Canada, 1969

IN the autumn of 1969 I received an invitation from John Power, a writer about the Canadian outdoors, to make a canoe trip with him through the wilderness of northeastern Ontario, paddling down the Yesterday River to the North French, then into the Moose River and down to Moose Factory on the shores of James Bay. 'I expect a rough go,' he wrote, and I knew him to be tough, 'with as many as a dozen portages a day.'

We flew to a place called Timmins with a mountain of gear. Gold was struck there in 1907. In 1964 it became a boom town for the second time when the Texas Sulphur Company made a major ore strike, and prospectors staked every inch of ground with more than twenty thousand claims in a wild mêlée.

When we got to Timmins I still had no boots, because I had just come from Bali. All the shops were shut but eventually I emerged from a cellar to which I had been guided with a pair of bright orange size twelves with steel caps, made especially for the locals, who are always dropping lumps of ore on their toes, by the Gorilla Boot Company.

Then we flew in a tiny Cessna to Cochrane, where there was an 8 p.m. curfew for people under sixteen. The weather was bad: ragged, smoking clouds spread across the horizon and there were violent rain squalls. Below us was the Boreal Forest, the Taiga, which extends without a break in a four-thousand-mile arc from Newfoundland to Alaska.

Next day we flew to what we were told was Rainy Lake on the Yesterday River in a De Havilland Beaver float plane. Down below rivers stretched away northward like steel springs under a mournful sky. But which was which?

At the lake, disembarkation took place on a boggy foreshore and during it the bag containing John's cameras and an immense back pack fell in the water.

There were four of us now: two Cree Indian trappers and food for an estimated ten-day journey down a river few people remembered anyone descending.

The two canoes had been flown in already, lashed to the floats of a plane. They were 17 feet long, built of chestnut with canvas skins and were not in good condition. One had been gnawed by a bear and the other had been holed in many places and not very expertly repaired.

Out on the lake a loon, a bird as big as a goose which can dive at 90 m.p.h., uttered an awful, demented cackle. It began to rain heavily and it was very cold. 'Going to snow,' one of the Crees said.

The Crees were phlegmatic, adept at overcoming disaster. Mine was called Johnny Smallboy. He had been a member of a Canadian tank crew at Cassino. John's was called Obadiah Trapper Junior. He was five feet tall and weighed fourteen stone, which meant that he was rectangular, and preferred to be called Spike.

The rations, put aboard at Cochrane at the last minute, were notably lacking in substance. There were only 2 lbs of jam, two tins of condensed milk, 4 lbs of sugar, no flour, except pancake mixture, no oatmeal, only one carton of matches. To make up the weight, however, there was an incredible quantity of fruit juice, potato mayonnaise and ketchup. The supplier had made what could possibly have been a fatal boob. Johnny Smallboy chose this moment to announce that neither he nor Spike had any tobacco. I told him that I would give them twenty cigarettes a day until supplies ran out. They ran out on the seventh day because they exceeded this ration.

The river was about fifty feet wide, the water black as jet and only about four feet deep. There were no sounds except the splash of the paddles and the cold north wind sighing in the tops of the spruce. There were no animals, no birds, not a sign of a fish. If this was the Yesterday it looked like its name; ghostly, gone. But after about five miles the Crees said it wasn't the Yesterday. We'd been landed on the wrong lake. This was the Wakwayowkastic which no white men and no Indians in living memory had ever been down so far as they knew. It went into the North French. Its name was a Cree word which meant 'River that Ends in the Sands'. The only stable thing on the map was the Seventh Base Line, a long, straight swathe cut through the forest for hundreds of miles from east to west by surveyors. If and when we ever crossed it we would know what latitude we were in.

The first camp was much like any other. The canoes were unloaded, run up on the foreshore and turned over. The Crees would fell a couple of dead trees with their 2½ lb axes and get a fire going in under five minutes, using wood shavings and one match. In thirty minutes Johnny had cooked dinner. Meanwhile, Spike lopped spruce boughs to make a soft bed under the groundsheets of the tents.

We wrote our journals by the light of a lamp made from the lid of a bully beef tin with melted lard in it and a piece of rag for a wick, the outfitter having omitted to provide oil lamps or candles.

The first night we had four speckled trout for dinner.

Dawn was about six-thirty, pale streaks of light against cobalt clouds. This was the time I liked best, warming myself by the fire, waiting for the tea, while Johnny told me about his life in the woods.

His wife was forty-four. She had had nine children and was now expecting another. When she had four children he used to take them up the North French by canoe to spend the winter at the trapping grounds. One child was born in the bush. He delivered it. In a good winter he reckoned to trap about 125 beaver, a dozen mink, 50–60 foxes, 60 marten and 75 muskrat. They lived off moose, snowshoe hares, grouse and beaver.

On the second day we came to the first rapids, a series of ten, three of them big ones, more than a mile long and very fast, with more rocks than water in them. Running them was exhilarating, going down at 20 m.p.h. in a haze of spray, the Crees in the sterns using big paddles, or long poles, and we in the bows pulling or paddling left or right to miss the rocks. We had to take care. As Spike said: 'Long walk Moose Factory. Maybe month, maybe more.'

When a canoe was holed we beached it and the Crees lit a fire, dried the bottom with a piece of burning wood and then plugged the holes with patent cement. When that ran out they used resin.

This was mid-September, the rutting season for moose, and on the second day we saw two magnificent bulls with antlers at the fullest stage of their development, called up by the Crees who could imitate any beast or bird. The third day was tougher. We made a portage over big falls, carrying the gear down on pack frames. As we went, everything we had began to collapse; rucksacks disintegrated, fibre boxes warped, cameras ceased to work, or were lost overboard.

In the forest there were red spruce now sixty or seventy feet high, and in the semi-darkness below, fallen trees lay like giants entombed in the deep green moss. The forest was inhabited by cheerful Canadian jays and we saw osprey, kingfishers and falcons. Beavers were splashing happily outside their lodges. At night the owls hooted madly and Canada geese rocketed upstream against the moon. Also on the banks were blood-sucking insects called no-sec-ums, giant mosquitoes and hordes of black fly.

We lost count of time and distance. It was difficult to know whether three miles or eight miles had been covered in a day when half of it was spent cutting a way through the bush, not on water at all. We never saw the Seventh Base Line.

The fifth, sixth, seventh, eighth and ninth days were the days of the long portages. Already, by this time, we had crossed three major falls and gone down 32 sets of rapids.

With their axes the Crees cut a path through the spruce and pine five feet wide and anything up to one and a half miles long, according to the length of the falls and rapids we were bypassing. Then they transported the canoes upside down with the paddles lashed inside, so that they could take some of the weight on their shoulders. Each canoe weighed 100 lbs, and they carried them fifty or sixty feet up the bank which had a gradient of about 1 in 3, then along the portage without stopping. After this they came back to help carry over the packs which weighed up to 120 lbs each.

It poured all through the day and night of the seventh and the portages were awful, but that night we dried out, more or less, before a big fire of cedar logs.

The big, final portage took one and a half days, out of sight of the river. We were very short of food now. Lunch on the eighth day was a slice of bread and bacon fat; dinner, soup made from ketchup with a slice of bread. We had little left now apart from tins and tins of orange juice and mayonnaise. There had been no time to hunt with the continual portaging and trout were elusive. That night Johnny took a shot at a beaver in the moonlight but missed.

The ninth day was better. After a breakfast of tea with orange juice in it and the last potatoes, the Crees, in spite of spending three hours cutting the last of the long portage, managed to kill three spruce grouse, two of them falling to Spike's catapult. That night we ate grouse stew.

On the tenth day we reached the mouth of the real Yesterday at noon, and in the afternoon came out in the North French, which was enormous in comparison with the Wakwayowkastic. Here we had a thin lunch, a spruce grouse between four of us.

The next morning, we set off while it was still dark, in a bitter wind which was coming off the Arctic Circle, down endless reaches with the islands in the river swathed in fog but with the tops of the trees looming above, like finials in a Gothic cathedral. Finally, after six hours, we rounded a bend and saw the Moose River stretching away to Moose Factory Island, Moosonee and the sea.

We landed at an Indian settlement where there were some dilapidated plywood huts on the edge of the forest, occupied by a few Cree families.

It was a sad place, with all the squalor of Western civilization but none of the amenities. Inside one of them Richard Angus Chechoo, aged seventy-four, one-time chief of a band of Crees, entertained us to tea, bread and butter and Spam. He had spent the first war in a Forestry unit at Virginia Water and he, too, like Johnny Smallboy, had spent his leave in Aberdeen.

We paddled on down into the beginning of the flood along the shores of interminable islands covered with scrub, with the wooden spire of the church on Moose Factory Island shining in the sun in the distance.

Then we had a long slog across the flooding tide in the main stream, towards Moosonee on the mainland. And then we were in by the jetty among the float planes and the now all-motorized canoes. No one paddled anymore.

As we landed a Canada goose came honking in over the little town, whose only communication with the outside world was by rail or air. Just like Spike, every Indian boy in Moosonee old enough to hold a catapult was out, and from all over the town came the honking of the children as they called to the goose to come down.

Richard Angus Chechoo, one-time Cree chieftain, with his squaw and grandson in a small settlement on the bank of the Moose River, northern Ontario.

Boat children, Aberdeen.

Already a port under the Mongols, otherwise the Yuan (1276–1368), what is now known as Aberdeen was one of the earliest settlements on Hong Kong Island. From it, in the time of the Ming (1368–1644), incense made from a plant known as *guan xiang*, which was grown on Tantau (otherwise Da yu Shan), a neighbouring island, was exported to the Yangtze valley. It was from this plant that what is now Aberdeen, and later the entire island, took the name Hong Kong, which is itself the transcription of the local pronunciation of *Xiang gang* – Incense Port. All rather complicated.

A Bubble in the South China Sea

Hong Kong, 1970

THE best time to go to Hong Kong is said to be in early winter – October to December – when there is a cool breeze, the sky is blue, and when the 90 per cent humidity of July and August is forgotten.

We arrived there in what is usually regarded as the no-good season, at the beginning of March. It was cloudy and rainy and cold enough most of the time to wear the great thick tweed suit I had brought, and was very glad I had brought, to wear in wintry Japan.

As we came in to land in cloud on the runway, there was not much to be seen of Hong Kong and its 235 adjacent islands, Kowloon and the New Territories; some bits of rock with surf pounding on them, part of a huge tenement block, a junk making heavy weather of it in the South China Sea.

It must have looked rather like this to the pilot of the aeroplane, too, because, next thing, we found ourselves disembarking hundreds of miles away at Manila in the Philippines, where the temperature was in the eighties, there was a riot in progress, and the local police were bowed down under the weight of endless belts of ammunition. None of the passengers complained much – after all it *was* a free trip and the Philippines were not somewhere you set off for on impulse.

Eventually, we landed at Hong Kong, and at the airport there were something like 12,000 people waiting to welcome our flight. Later, an official told me that this was the entire complement of some dozen

Chinese families who had turned up, as apparently Chinese families invariably do, *en masse* to welcome a dozen or so relatives who were disembarking from our plane. If there had been more locals on board there would have been even more people to meet them.

Then, having told the customs official that we were not importing any liquor, tobacco, hydrocarbon oils, methyl alcohol or table water – I can't remember the whole lot – which were all dutiable because this was a Free Port in which you were supposed to stock up on such commodities, not spoil the market in them, we were whisked away in a shiny, rather ancient Rolls-Royce, by an equally shiny, equally ancient Chinese driver, the only one who had come to meet us. This machine was equipped with locally built air-conditioning so effective that it was as cold as a haunted house, but fortunately there was a fur rug on the floor in case we had forgotten our boots.

We whirred through Kowloon in the Rolls without stopping in Kowloon City, a weird, six-acre slum, which had walls until the Japanese broke them down during their occupation. The inhabitants of the city have always considered it and themselves part of China proper, and in 1963 Peking made a formal claim for it.

Then we drove on to the *Star* ferry. Ahead rose the fantastic, unforgettable façade of the City of Victoria on Hong Kong Island, full of looming white monoliths, like huge teeth with lots of fillings in them (high-rise buildings, actually), while somewhere above and behind them were the upper parts of the island, now invisible under a thick, lop-sided wig of grey nimbus.

This was not what it had looked like until recently, if one was to believe all those tinted, panoramic photographs to be seen in every second Chinese restaurant in Britain. In these photographs there had been lots of white-washed four- and five-storeyed buildings, with verandas on each storey on which white-suited merchants had taken their ease overlooking the ground of the Hong Kong Cricket Club. When some of those pictures were taken the largest buildings had been those of the Hong Kong and Shanghai Banking Corporation, built in the 1930s, and one or two similarly important ones such as the headquarters of Jardine Matheson, a merchant firm which was functioning before the foundation of Hong Kong but which lost a packet when Red China took over their mainland interests in the 1950s.

Now the houses were gone, no one wore white trousers any more, except sailors, the cricket pitch was on the point of being built over, although the Hong Kong Club, the Supreme Court building and Jardine Matheson's still remained as reminders of the old hierarchical order, while up above, on the Peak, were the lovely homes in which the administrators still lived, as they always had, hidden for months on end, as they currently were, in their own personal cloud, which may have been one of the reasons why policy in this part of the world sometimes seemed a bit obfuscated. There was nothing Eastern about Victoria at all, architecturally speaking.

But on the water this was still the East. There was no doubt about that. Out at the moorings on both sides of the Central Fairway, the deep channel which led out towards the South China Sea, there were dozens of merchant ships with their riding lights just coming on, in what was the Hong Kong winter equivalent of a Scottish gloaming. Cargoes were being put in and out of them, and the harbour was full of lighters and junks and sampans and boats called Walla Wallas, which you rode in after a party when the last ferry had gone; and the air was filled with outlandish cries and the most disturbing sound in all the world, that of ships' sirens announcing their imminent departure for Port Swettenham, Saigon, Pointe Noire, Okinawa, Lautoka, Khorramshahr, Galveston and the Piraeus, just some of the places that the Hong Kong newspapers listed each day in its shipping news under arrivals and departures.

Then we rolled off the ferry and up to the door of the Mandarin Hotel, one of the larger and taller monoliths. Perhaps it was usual for the rich to be met at the airport by one of the two hotel Rolls, though what happened when a bevy of rich people arrived on the same flight, all expecting the Rolls treatment, goodness only knows.

There, we were met by a Sikh commissionaire in red boots, who looked as if he could have done with a spell on the barracks square, an immensely tall head porter, who looked rather like a worldly sort of bishop, an assistant manager and The Manager, late of the Savoy, who apologized for the absence of someone else (God, presumably), all of which struck us both as awe-inspiring, indeed.

That is all about the Mandarin. it might not have had the best food in the world, few good hotels do; but it was a lap of luxury and it did have wonderful service, and during our entire stay no one said, 'You're welcome!' If you wanted that there was a

Below
The waterfront, Aberdeen, where the junks come from Red China unloaded. A Tanka woman navigating in the rain.

Overleaf
Junks at Aberdeen, 1970.

One of the most rewarding things you could do in Hong Kong was simply to sit on the waterfront at Aberdeen and watch the thousands of Tankas, boat people, going about their daily life aboard their junks and sampans. It was like being on the edge of a dense sub-tropical forest in which masts took the place of trees, rigging took the place of creepers, and the canvas tilts erected on the decks below were the roofs of the houses. Here, in an area in which typhoons are commonplace – about twenty-five a year – both boats and people were in relative safety. One of the worst typhoons was in September, 1937, which stranded 28 ocean-going liners, sank 1250 junks and drowned 11,000 people.

In those days, with the Cultural Revolution (1965–68) only recently at an end, I looked with awe across the Shum Chun river at the wire entanglements and watch towers of the People's Republic. In this region a more immediate hazard was presented by the women of a tribe known as Hakkas, meaning, literally, 'strangers'. A hardy and frugal race, the Hakkas lived mostly in the hilly parts. Of terrifying aspect, they wore huge straw hats edged with what looked like black curtains, ostensibly to keep the sun off their faces. Ever since the time when photography was in its infancy, the Hakka women had resisted any attempts to photograph them; but then, all of a sudden, they woke up to the commercial possibilities of posing for tourists, and those who didn't want to avail themselves of this facility were now driven up the wall by them.

Overleaf
Construction work, Aberdeen. Even twenty years ago, big developments were on the go everywhere. As you drove into Aberdeen there was a Chinese temple on the roadside where you could have your fortune told for a consideration. I wonder if it's still there? I wonder what has happened to Aberdeen? Perhaps it's better not to know.

Hilton higher up the hillside. In fact although the Mandarin looked rather American, it was strictly Chinese-British.

If you wanted to be even more British at that time, you could stay in Kowloon in a room with a view at the Peninsula Hotel on Tsimshatsui Point, near the place where the *Star* ferry took off for Hong Kong Island. It was built in 1926 to house travellers waiting to set off on, or descending from, the Canton railway on the first stretch of their journey to London.

Installed in a room at the Mandarin sufficiently expensive to make it seem extravagant to take one's eyes off the unparalleled views, the problem was what to see of the rest of the colony in the time – only five days – at our disposal. We needed this time, and much more, to satisfy our curiosity about the place. For instance, we wanted to admire the view from the top of the Peak. Fortunately, we were saved from having to decide whether it was one of the half dozen greatest views on earth by the cloud that continued to obliterate it; but we still needed time to find out, for example, whether it was true that 80,000 people at that time really did live on the rooftops of crumbling tenements; what it was like inside one of the vast new resettlement blocks (was there really only one lavatory to each floor, 400 people to a floor, four to a ten-by-ten-foot room?); if coolies, in 1970, were still really getting less than HK$50 a week for a twelve-hour day, when HK$1 was equal to about 1s.2d. (about 6p); whether the prostitutes who operated in the sampans in the typhoon anchorage really were all blind, and why.

We also wanted time to sit on a packing case on the waterfront at Aberdeen and watch the boat people, when the term 'boat people' had a happier connotation, living their happier lives on junks and sampans, their small children with a rope round their waists to stop them falling over the side; time to investigate the markets in narrow lanes and eat in restaurants rarely visited by Europeans, but to which they were not refused admission, only admitted with a certain wonderment (Hong Kong had the best Chinese food outside Peking and Taiwan); time to visit the places where they sold Sung dynasty ceramics taken from burial grounds outside China, and the big Chinese republican emporia, communist bastions at the heart of capitalism, and doing so wonder how on earth they could sell hand-crocheted double bedspreads for £6, which would take a young woman with the keenest eyesight a minimum of a month to make.

A lot of time was needed: to have your horoscope cast in a temple; to journey by train – on the hard seats preferably – up towards the frontier, towards the New Territories, parts of which looked as rural as we imagined, without having seen it, rural China must still look; to peer out across the duck ponds towards the watch towers on the border river at Lok Ma Chau, where we were driven nearly nuts by the attentions of beggar ladies of the Hakka tribe (who wear big black hats with deep fringes and look like a get-together of female mutes); time to visit the street where they sold wholesale aphrodisiacs, where it was probably more expensive to buy the ground-up horns of the animals than the entire beast itself; time to try out the banal nightlife in the girlie bars, dozens and dozens of them; and to visit the film studios where some 120 film companies churned out about 300 films a year in Mandarin and Cantonese.

And at least one day had to be kept for an excursion to Macau, about

forty miles away across the mouth of the Pearl River to the west, 75 minutes by hydrofoil. The city itself stands on a peninsula only two miles square, joined to an island, which is part of China, by a narrow isthmus, and there are also a couple of other islands. The whole territory only adds up to six square miles.

Macau, officially, was Portuguese and had its own governor, but its independence from China was, in fact, even more tenuous than that of Hong Kong. Carefully engineered riots at the time of the Cultural Revolution reduced the administration to such a state of sycophancy that anyone the People's Republic asked for by name was almost certainly handed over without argument. Nevertheless, it was not nearly as dangerous to visit as it sounded as the Chinese had never been known to ask for tourists, and it was still a place with the most attractively decadent air about it, although of what its decadence actually consisted was a bit of a mystery.

Even its principal exports had something exotic about them – Chinese wine and medicines, incense sticks, firecrackers and other fireworks, some of them dangerous, matches, camphor and teakwood chests, and gold ingots which came from God knows where but were then thought to be smuggled to Hong Kong.

The fish market, Aberdeen.

A few seconds after this picture was taken, someone took all our travellers' cheques from a buttoned, inside pocket. Not only these but also the key to the hotel safe at the Mandarin Hotel. I had to pay a bomb to get another one flown out from England.

Built on seven hills, but otherwise not at all like Rome, except perhaps morally, Macau had the most hideous hotel if not in the world, in the East – built for the comfort of the Japanese who swarmed into Macau at certain seasons, the city and the hotel being famous for their gambling. In the entrance hall there was an immense chandelier that could be raised and lowered by a mechanism of such complexity that when they needed to clean it they had to get a man out from Germany to work it.

Much nicer was the Bela Vista, a splendidly decrepit place with cast-iron staircases and a wonderful view over a bay crowded with sampans, the Praia Grande, in which I would have been happy to spend the rest of my days, providing I wasn't forcibly removed to the People's Republic, drinking the good Portuguese wine. The Bela Vista was a mirror of the whole city, which was indeed almost totally decrepit, with row upon row of lovely old houses painted in faded colours, some equally lovely old churches and a fantastic Renaissance cathedral, at the top of a long flight of steps, of which only the façade remained.

Flying back towards Hong Kong in the hydrofoil across the mouth of the Pearl River, which had eight times the discharge of the Yellow River and was all discoloured with silt, with dozens of junks surging down it from Canton on the wind; and having put our money on zero on the big table in the big hotel and recouped thirty-five times our stake by doing so, and with the islands ahead rushing up out of the sea to meet us, we both felt that this was quite enough for just one short day.

A Tanka child on the waterfront, Aberdeen.

A peasant woman on market day,
Oxkutzcab.

In the Realms of Yucatan
Mexico, 1971

THE name Yucatan only came into use after 1528 when the Castilian conquistador Don Francesco de Montejo took possession of the more accessible parts of the hinterland in the name of the King of Spain. He and his successors got little out of the country. There was no metal of any kind, let alone gold and silver, and nothing like enough local inhabitants to make it economically exploitable by Spanish slave-driving standards.

'Ouyouckatan!' ('Just listen to them') the Mayans are reputed to have exclaimed on first hearing the Castilian dialect, and this is why it is called Yucatan, although savants with their usual dreary pedantry have insisted that it means Land of the Yuca, a cassava that was used to make a sort of bread, and tapioca. Both versions are probably wrong. In what was the land of the Mayans anything was possible.

Most visitors to Yucatan flew from Mexico City to Merida, the capital, in about 1½ hours. Or you could cover the 945 miles from Mexico City by bus in about 22 hours, or by train in 36 hours (Pullman and dining car service). To further the illusion that this really was a voyage of discovery we chose to arrive by sea, at Progreso, the principal port.

On either side of a 2000-metre-long jetty white beaches with palms behind stretched away seemingly for ever. The *nortes*, otherwise the *temporales*, were blowing and the sea was steaming up on them and spraying the windows of the bijou and not-so-bijou but uniformly hideous villas of the well-to-do Meridans who fled here from the capital in July and August – months in which Merida was to be avoided like the Black Death, as this was the rainy season and every afternoon its streets were turned into canals on which no one had thought of running a boat service. The best time to go to Yucatan is from October to March when the day temperature is around 70°F to 80°F and the nights are cool, around 60°F.

Offshore at Progreso the sea is infested with man-eating sharks, at least it was in 1911 when my copy of Terry's *Guide to Mexico*, signed by the author, was published, and what Terry said was good enough for me. Swimming was safe from the beaches.

Progreso was a straggling place only a few streets deep from front to back, so you had to be careful not to penetrate too far or you ended up in a swamp. There were some semi-open-air fish restaurants and some atmospheric drinking places with swing doors with barrels painted on them in case you couldn't read, and there was a lot of sand about, most of it airborne.

From Progreso the principal crop of the country, *henequén*, otherwise sisal, was exported, but the business was in a pretty terrible way because of the use of synthetics, and so was the trade in *chicle*, I was glad to hear, the other principal export – the loathsome base of chewing gum which makes sitting down anywhere such a hazardous business, some maniac having recently discovered a substitute for that, too.

There are two sorts of Yucatezos:

pure-blooded Mayans, a minority, whose menfolk in particular often bear a striking resemblance to the sculptures of their ancestors in their ruined cities; and the Mestizos (the women are Mestizas), who are a mixture of Mayan and Spanish. The Yucatezos are among the most handsome of the Mexican peoples. They have beautiful manners and are very hospitable, and profess a fervent Catholicism on to which they have grafted more ancient beliefs.

The women have jet-black eyes, and equally black hair caught up at the back in a bun and finished off with a bow. They wear the *huipil*, here called the *ipil*, a long white cotton shift with a square neck, neck and hem being embroidered with brilliant flowers. Below the hem of some of the shorter ones a lace-trimmed underskirt could sometimes be glimpsed.

It was only 24 miles from Progreso to Merida and the road was dead straight. At first it ran on a causeway across an enormous, eerie lagoon full of mangrove trees, many of them dead and bleached white. Beyond these swamps was The Interior – flat as a pancake, composed of limestone, which formed the foundation of the entire peninsula, with a minimum of earth on top. In it grew endless plantations of greeny grey *hene-quén* plants. From the white-fibred sort the Mayans made the ropes used to haul the blocks of stone up the steep sides of their enormous pyramids.

Occasionally we passed a grove of palm and casuarina trees which meant that almost certainly there was a *cenote* nearby. A *cenote* is a water-filled cave, sometimes one in which the roof has collapsed, leaving a large hole open to the sky. They can be of truly arcadian beauty.

There are no surface rivers in Yucatan. They all run underground.

The *cenotes* supply the water and in the country are often used as bathing places. The Mayans used them for ritual purposes, sometimes of a bloodthirsty nature. The giant *cenote* at Chichén Itzá is said to have been used as a propitiatory dumping place for auspiciously cross-eyed virgins who were drowned in it. After a short time in Yucatan one begins to suspect that Cecil B. de Mille must have been a Mayan.

Finally we arrived in Merida, where whole streets of Spanish colonial houses were being torn down to make room for office blocks. In spite of this there were still sufficient to give the place a remarkable quality. In Merida the streets formed a grid at right angles to one another, and originally each *calle* was identifiable by an ideograph, the *calle* of the elephant by an elephant, that of the flamingo by an oversize flamingo, and so on.

Now they were numbered, odd numbers from east to west, even from north to south. This, with the superimposition of a one-way street system, was enough to make visitors throw away their motor cars, which was probably what was intended. By far the best thing was to clip-clop down to the markets in one of the old, horse-drawn *calesas* in search of a straw hat, some of which were so fine that they could be drawn through a ring.

The old Spanish houses had a distinctly Moorish look. They had thick walls washed in delicate pastel greens, blues and pinks. Very often they had roof gardens and always a white tank for catching rain water for drinking, and a windmill, of which there were estimated to be between 15,000 and 20,000 in the city, for drawing up washing water from the depths below. The tall, narrow windows were covered with delicate iron grilles. Inside the heavy

Cities of the quick and dead.

doors which opened on to the street there was an arcaded patio with flowers, climbing plants and palms growing, and often there was a fountain. Big hammocks swung from wooden knobs set in the walls of the arcades. Everyone in Yucatan slept in a hammock. Even in Merida the use of a bed, except by foreigners and in hotels, was almost unknown.

The best *hamacas* were made from the white sisal fibre and were incredibly fine, like lace. They lasted forever and were correspondingly expensive. *Hamacas matrimoniales* held entire families. Yucatezos are conceived, born and die in *hamacas*. Among the best in Merida were those made by the female inmates of the penitentiary. They welcomed visitors, but their *hamacas* were no cheaper.

'How do you make love in a *hamaca*?' I asked a gentleman in the city. He laughed, gave his moustaches a twirl, and said, 'It is necessary to keep one foot on the ground.'

And now, having found out what to do in order not to loop the loop while making love in a *hamaca*, we set off for the ruins, which is what the majority of visitors come to see.

Having visited them I despaired of writing about them. How could one write about what one had only dimly apprehended; about Chichén Itzá, Uxmal, and the enormous and to me (apart from a beautiful *cenote* in which we swam) uninspiring Dzichibaltun, which covers about 30 acres and has 8000 unexcavated structures in it? We knew what they must have looked like when new, from drawings and models and what the Spaniards wrote about them when they had scarcely had time to decay. The squares were perfectly paved; the dazzlingly polished buildings, the number of columns, the staircases and even the number of times some sculptural feature was reiterated, all expressed their involvement with the measurement and the passing of time. These, and the pyramids and the observatories that enabled them to measure to 0.00069 of a day, the length of a solar year, could be seen for miles towering above the jungle trees, all built by people who had no knowledge of the keystone arch and without the aid of the wheel or metal instruments of any kind.

But in spite of their brilliance and erudition I could not rid myself of the feeling that the Mayans and the Toltecs who encroached on their territories had something slightly Hollywoodish about them. I knew they worshipped gods of the earth, moon and stars and the hideous, snouted Chac, god of water, and we had seen the reclining Chac-Mools, great reclining stone monoliths into whose laps the hearts of the sacrificial victims were thrown after they had been scooped from their bodies with obsidian knives.

Both the Mayans and the Toltecs seem to have been a cold, organization-man lot. The Mayans played a game called *pok-ta-pok* in enormous open courts using a ball made from the ubiquitous *chicle*, a game that sometimes involved the slaughter of numbers of the losing side. I always hated team games, anyway.

It was the pleasure of ruins in the sense that Rose Macaulay wrote about them that would have led us to return if we had the chance. We preferred by far the more ruined places to those that had been made almost as good as new and were tended by devoted custodians who mowed the lawns and pulled up the shoots sent out by the trees and creepers in the surrounding jungle, which, given the opportunity, would engulf them yet again.

Opposite
El Castillo, a Mayan pyramid, Chichén Itzá.

Overleaf
The Great Tree of Tule, in the churchyard of *La Virgen de la Asunción* on the road from Oaxaca to Mitla, in Mexico. The largest in Mexico, a sort of cypress (*Taxodium distichum*), the tree was some two thousand years old and 160 feet high. Four feet above the ground it was 160 feet in circumference, and the spread of its branches was 140 feet. In its shade Hernan Cortés and his soldiers took a siesta while *en route* to Honduras.

Young Fijians, of whom there were inexhaustible supplies, all pelting down the road after us and shouting, 'Ullo! Ullo!'

Divine Archipelago
Fiji, 1971

UNTIL I went there, I thought – if I had ever thought about it – that Fiji was a single island such as Corsica, St Helena or the Isle of Wight. Now I know that it is an archipelago of more than 800 islands which altogether are about the size of Wales scattered over about a hundred thousand square miles of the South Pacific, and that they are so close to the 180th Meridian, which is also the International Date Line, that it actually passes through one of them, the island of Taveuni, on which a monument records this strange, nineteenth-century invention whereby you lose or gain a day of earthly pleasures when going round the world from West to East or vice-versa.

Why did we choose to go to Fiji when there were so many other islands and archipelagos of islands in the Pacific on which you could smell such characteristic smells as those of copra, the scent of unidentifiable exotic flowers, the incenses of religions that were not always Christian; witness fantastic sunsets and dawns which were like the creation of the world all over again, and on which you could listen to the trade wind humming in the high tops of the coconut palms, the sound of the surf booming on the reefs out beyond the turquoise lagoons and on the dazzling beaches; and also hear the buzzing of flies, the demented howl of the non-malarial mosquito and the strange nocturnal cries of birds in the dark forests behind the coast, which suggested a mysterious and probably untouristy interior?

Because it was the only way,

unless they happened to be fighting world wars, or playing rugby, about which they were crazy, in Sydney, Auckland, Swansea or Twickenham, of seeing the Fijians themselves.

Fijians were charming and good-humoured – when they laughed, which was pretty incessantly, the noise sounded as if it emanated from where their boots would have been had they worn any. They were handsome rather than beautiful (the men looked like great standing stones, the girls were comely and come-hither). The red light section of Suva, the capital on Viti Levu, was a farce. Nobody used it.

They were also generous to a degree which might be regarded as excessive: an ancient custom known as *kerekere* obliged a Fijian to hand over any possession fancied by another Fijian, who simply had to ask for it. This made it impossible for them to engage in shopkeeping with any hope of success, since the stock was simply removed from the shelves by relatives and friends as soon as it came in. This, without any suggestion of payment on their part or, indeed, any being demanded.

The Fijians had been described to me as lazy. In fact they were an extremely skilful people and indisputably the best boat and house builders in the entire Pacific. They were, and probably still are, however, convinced of the stupidity of any kind of repetitive labour beyond that which satisfied their immediate needs.

Consequently, they were the des-pair of the British colonial administrators who were in charge of them until 1970 and who undoubtedly loved them. It was then that Fiji became an independent state and a member of the Commonwealth, with a Governor-General appointed by the Queen.

Those who didn't love them were the businessmen who imported cheap, indentured Hindu labour into the country to harvest sugar cane. The result was that by 1971 there were more Indians than Fijians in Fiji, none of whom had any intention of returning to the land of their forefathers, most of whom had never seen it, anyway, and by that time had long since ceased to be serfs and were now well-off farmers, shopkeepers and, worst of all, moneylenders to the Fijians. All this constituted a terrible problem for the Fijians, now in nominal control of their country, which they had no idea how to solve.

Subjected to their disingenuous charm, I found it difficult to believe that the solution to their problems might be of a sanguinary nature. Yet not much more than one hundred years previously, the Fijians were world-famous for their bloodthirstiness, treacherous natures and anthropophagous habits. Suspicious even of their nextdoor neighbours, they lived in villages perched on inaccessible ridges. They were noted for pelting one another with specially selected stones the size of cricket balls (not surprising that, after rugby, cricket is their favourite game), strangling their nearest relatives as a mark of respect on the death of a person of greater importance, burying people under the corner posts of newly constructed houses, and, above all, eating one another in truly enormous quantities. These islands were not called the Cannibal Isles for nothing.

One chief without any help from his friends consumed 999 people (presumably keeping the thousandth as a form of iron ration) and every time he ate one he erected a stone pillar as a sort of aide-mémoire. Fijians ate anyone who came to hand not because they believed, as the members of some primitive societies do, that the consumer gained some of the innate qualities of the consumed, but simply because they enjoyed eating what they called 'long pig'.

For this purpose they used multipronged wooden forks, instruments that were still on offer secondhand but which I had no interest in acquiring.

In these circumstances, in these islands, on what was virtually a *route des gastronomes*, no one was safe, shipwrecked sailors meeting the same fate as the men and women of alien tribes who had strayed a little too far from home. Such was the turnover that an island on which we stopped, which was regarded as the Fijian Pantheon, had been raised several feet above its original level by human bones. On them we passed the night of our twenty-fifth wedding anniversary.

The miraculous change of heart which had turned the Fijians into one of the friendliest races in the Pacific (travelling anywhere it was obligatory to wave to every single man, woman and child met with *en route*) must, reluctantly, be attributed to the efforts of the missionaries – Wesleyans, Seventh Day Adventists, Roman Catholics (known rather charmingly as *Popi*), Church of England and other sects in descending order of successful conversion rates – and also of their proselytes, some of whom were extremely courageous.

It is strange that with one exception missionaries were the only people who were never eaten, although they used to complain con-

Young Fijian in camouflage? Ambush?

stantly to the chiefs in whose territories they resided about the smoke from the open-cast ovens which were often situated embarrassingly close to their places of worship.

The exception was a Wesleyan, the Reverend Thomas Baker, who was cooked and eaten, boots and all, together with a number of converts who acted as side dishes, near the headwaters of the Singatoka River, in July 1867.

At the time of our visit, in the 1970s, a Fijian village had anything between twenty and five hundred inhabitants, and the houses, which often stood beneath ancient trees, were grouped around a large, grassy open space, called the *rara*, which was used for ceremonies. It resembled an old-fashioned English village green plonked down in the tropics. This was where the house of the chief would be, the *vale levu*, and although all the houses were raised above the ground on platforms of earth or stones, his would be the most elevated. Bigger villages had a cricket and football pitch as well.

When invited to enter one of these houses, as they surely would be if they showed signs of wishing to do so, visitors removed their shoes at the entrance.

If it was an old house it would have a thatched roof and it would be built of wood and reeds and decorated with sinnet, a sort of flat, plaited cordwork. Otherwise it might have a corrugated-iron roof because house building, as was every other domestic activity of the Fijians, was communal, and now that more people went away to work in towns it was more difficult to find enough of them to do the thatching.

Then they washed their feet in a wooden bowl and squatted down on the floor which was upholstered with grass and covered with beautiful mats made from a sort of pine leaf, or else from sedges.

Everything was very simple. On one side there was a raised sleeping platform; on another an open fireplace, but no chimney. There might also be one or two pieces of furniture.

The owner of the house then offered the visitors half a coconut shell which contained *yanggona*. If the shell was an old one, it had a sort of bluish bloom on it as if it had been enamelled.

Yanggona, the *kava* of some other South Sea islands, is made by dissolving the green root of a shrub, *Piper methysticum*, which has been pulped on a rough volcanic stone, in cold water.

The best roots are about five years old. Alternatively, it is prepared with the dried root which is powdered in a mortar. The root is a more or less obligatory gift and all visitors to Fijian houses provided themselves with a good stock of it, either in powder or vegetable form. It is the idea of the gift that is important to Fijians.

It was also a good idea to bring a couple of bottles of rum for the moment when the *yanggona* ran out.

In the past, young bachelors and nubile girls used to prepare the *yanggona* by chewing the green root, a practice that by the time we got here had fallen into disuse. It was much more potent made in this way.

Before we took the proffered drink we clapped our hands slowly and intoned the words '*Ni Mbula*' ('Good health'), and when we had drunk it the other people present clapped their hands and exclaimed, '*A Matha*' ('It is dry').

The taste of *yanggona* has been compared to soapy water with a dash of peppermint added, some say pepper, others rhubarb that has been mixed with magnesia and flavoured with sal volatile, not a mixture in which most of us have indulged very frequently. The effect on the palate is rather like having one's mouth lined with tissue paper, or the effect of a pain-killing injection.

Personally, I thought it looked like dirty washing-up water and tasted of *yanggona*, but after the tissue paper/ Novocaine effect had worn off I felt cool, refreshed and in the mood for more.

Apparently, you don't get drunk on *yanggona*, it only makes you want to smoke and pee. The paralysis of the lower limbs which is alleged to supervene after overindulgence, proceeds solely from the excruciatingly uncomfortable position you are required to assume in order to drink it. So much for *yanggona*.

On and Off the Shores of the Spanish Main

West Indies, 1972

'*Bonne chance*,' said the indefatigable Air France stewardess. She had looked after us *en route* from Martinique. Now she seemed genuinely reluctant that we should disembark at Port-au-Prince.

Inside the airport building we joined a queue which ultimately brought us to a desk at which was perched a large man of about fifty wearing dark glasses and an unseasonably thick Cheviot suit. It required no effort of the imagination to identify this senior citizen as a former member of *Les Volontaires de la Sécurité Nationale*, otherwise the *Tontons Macoutes*, an organization that, with the passing of Papa Doc two years previously, was now under a temporary cloud. Some eight thousand of these Bogeymen were said to be building roads in remote places, but not all of them.

'Visitor's Card two US dollar!'

I told him that I had French francs, English pounds, West Indian dollars and sterling traveller's cheques, but to each of these offerings in turn he said, 'No! Two US dollar!'

I eventually persuaded this individual, who, apart from his dark glasses, almost bullet-proof suit and limited gift of tongue, resembled one of the larger primates, to allow me through the barriers to cash a cheque. It was a Sunday and there was no one to do it, but finally a hovering taximan gave me some dollars in exchange for pounds, which he did at an appallingly adverse rate.

Back in 'Immigration' I gave the ex-*Tonton Macoute* two US dollars; he put the notes in an inside pocket, not in the suitcase in which I had watched him deposit most, but not all, of the money he received from the other temporary immigrants.

Now he showed signs of leaving. 'Hey!' I said, indignantly, 'what about my Visitor's Card?' He gave me the sort of inscrutable look which you only get from people who wear dark glasses, then vanished through a door marked 'No Admittance'. Also prominently displayed was a sign bearing the words, 'BUSINESS MEN! MAKE YOUR STAY IN HAITI PROFITABLE BY PUTTING ON A BUSINESS!'

By the time we reached the customs hall the customs officers had made off, too. No need, while I was on the plane, to jettison my maps and Graham Greene's *The Comedians*. In the hall, abandoned, I found a coffee table book entitled *Haiti. The First Negro Republic in the World. Its True Face*, printed, as the blurb said, 'By Private Initiative'.

The one who had provided this initiative had now gone, but his totally unmemorable visage still peered out in a colour photograph from page 13, with a framed portrait of Pope Paul on the mantelshelf behind him: Papa Doc, Eighth President for Life, now officially known as 'Le Grand Disparu'. Looking at his photograph it was difficult to imagine that he had had the head of an opponent hewn from his shoulders, flown to him from an outlying *département* in a bucket of ice, placed in a deep freeze in his palace, and then, from time to time, brought to him after office hours so that he could contemplate it in his 'in' tray during the steamy watches of the night.

The Grand Hotel Oloffson, Port-au-Prince, Haiti.

At around 6.30 every evening, César the barman began circulating the rum punches to those members of the literary and theater (*sic*) sets who described the place as 'darling'; and to exquisite members of the local smart set, whose patrician countenances ranged in pigmentation from the jet black of Africa to the palest of *sangmêlées* (nowhere else in the Caribbean, rich or poor, could you see more beautiful people). And there was M. Aubelin Joliecoeur – the 'Petit Pierre' of Greene's *Comedians*, much of which was set in the Oloffson – a tiny, posturing, white-silk-suited, chocolate-coloured journalist and PR man to the regime; here, there and everywhere, waving a little cane, calling people he had never met, including us, 'darling', and from time to time popping out to bully his chauffeur.

At last, after a discussion about the fare, difficult to sustain in the red-hot wind that was blowing, and on an empty stomach (and because it was the only remaining taxi), we entered 'my' taximan's taxi – the one who had changed my pounds for me – a huge, black, hearse-like Steinbergian vehicle, and were driven off down what had been intended as a triumphal avenue and eventually into Avenue Dessalines, otherwise La Grande Rue, which runs through the heart of the city, leaving on the right La Route du Fort Dimanche.

The Fort was marked on an oil company's map, picked up free of charge at the airport, as *lieu d'intérêt*. Interesting, presumably, because few prisoners had ever emerged from it in one piece. In the middle of the night, Le Grand Disparu took his son-in-law, the husband of his eldest daughter, to the Fort and forced him to witness, as a mark of disapproval of the daughter's marriage to such a potentially dangerous army officer, the execution of nineteen of his own friends by an impromptu firing squad composed of fellow officers.

Later, we sat on the veranda of the Grand Hotel Oloffson in Port-au-Prince, having consumed a delicious light luncheon served by an old retainer who answered to the name of C'est Dieu. As we found it imposs-ible to hail him by this name, or even to paraphrase it, we contented our-selves with attracting his attention in the English manner, that is by raising a hand weakly and calling out, 'Er . . . !' or 'I say . . . !'

This was the hotel of Greene's *The Comedians*, and from where we were sitting we could see the swimming pool, down in a corner of the tropical garden, in which, empty in the novel, some minister or other had rather messily done away with him-self. Now, full of water, it looked positively inviting.

The hotel stood on the lush lower slopes of Kenscoff Mountain, which, particularly towards evening, looms over the city in a somewhat alarm-ing manner, as if it were about to fall and squash it flat. A truly astonish-ing structure – in a country in which this epithet has become meaningless from sheer overuse – the hotel was originally built to house Simon Sam, President of Haiti from 1896 to 1902 – not to be confused with his name-sake, Guillaume Sam, also President, who ended up being impaled by a mob on the railings of the French Embassy in 1915, after which he was torn to pieces.

It was the embellishments of the Oloffson that made it unique. Built of almost indestructible mahogany and painted a sizzling white, from every possible and impossible van-tage point it sprouted turrets, spires, crotchets, finials and balconies, some of which appeared to have been put on upside down, all of them riddled with fretwork to such an extent that it seemed a miracle that it could remain standing. It was as if some giant, but inspired, wood-boring insect had been let loose on a solid, decent, colonial clapboard structure.

Oriental was what it was, the sort of orient suggested in Coleridge's spectacular visions of Xanadu. The bar with the brilliant colours of the primitive Haitian paintings shining through the perpetual dusk of day-time, the dining room with its rocks and greenery could well have been the ante chambers to caverns leading down to a sunless sea, which was exactly what the visitor craved for after a morning's sightseeing in the inferno of Port-au-Prince.

Behind the hotel was a ram-shackle, circular construction with a corrugated-iron roof which was rather like an open umbrella. Below it hundreds of pairs of black and off-black feet could be seen dangling. This was a *gaguère*, a cockpit, and the owners of the feet were the spectators. Inside, it was like an engraving by Hogarth, but one in which all the protagonists were black. Large sums of money were changing hands and *clairin*, the cheapest and rawest spirit, was circulating.

Soon a main, a cockfight, began on the beaten earth of the *gaguère*. The birds did not wear steel spurs. There was no need; their own were sharpened so that they were like stilettos. We knew from accounts of the *gaguère* by other visitors to Haiti that we weren't going to enjoy it, and when one bird had had one of its wings partly torn off and the other was eyeless we left.

The following morning, as it grew progressively hotter, we walked down into Port-au-Prince through lanes flaming with bougainvillea. Passers-by said '*Bonjour, blancs*' in a friendly way, a pleasant change from Dominica where we had been told 'Go home, whites!' three times in fifteen minutes.

On the way we saw some of the principal sights: among them the tomb of Le Grand Disparu, which looked like a bijou villa in an enormous dazzlingly-white cemetery, guarded by sentries who also looked after the gas cylinder which provided gas for the perpetual flame; and an enormous hoarding on which was displayed, several times larger than life, the figure of Jean-Paul Duvalier, the Doctor's obese son, Ninth President for Life, in full evening dress, with the banner headline *L'Idole du Peuple*.

Then on, past the Palace (no stopping), into the dilapidated heart of the city by the Grande Rue, the air lethally heavy with the exhaust fumes of a thousand deep-laden *camionettes* – the gaudily painted vehicles of the public bus system – to the Iron Market, having been asked by every second person in the Grande Rue if we would give them a dollar, although they showed no hope of receiving anything at all.

In the market you could buy, among other things, lampshades made of shiny tin, clay pipes which were smoked by women in the interior, and locally made brassieres. Brassieres, baseballs, textiles, instant divorces and blood plasma, bought from the already anaemic inhabitants at $3 a litre, were at that time some of the most thriving exports to the United States, from a country in which the legal wage of manual workers was $1 a day (no wonder American big business was attracted to Haiti).

Up the hill, by the cathedral, poor women dressed in white, indistinguishable from the ecstatic devotees who crowded the *tonnelles* (the Voodoo peristyles) at night, knelt on the pavement before the shrines with their arms outstretched imploringly, or else they clung to the railings as if the Devil was trying to drag them away. Or was it Baron Samedi, Lord of the Cemeteries and Chief of the Legion of the Dead, in his frock coat, bowler hat and carrying a black walking stick, who was doing the dragging? To whom were these women addressing themselves? The Christian Trinity and the saints, or the gods of Africa: Bon-Dieu-Bon, otherwise Le Grand Maître, who is sometimes male and sometimes female, Ogoun Feraile, God of War, Bossu Comblamin, or the Virgin of the Seven Sorrows, or St Rose of Lima in their other guises?

In Haiti, Catholicism and Voodooism are so inextricably mixed in the minds of the people that many Catholic priests, after strenuous but totally unsuccessful attempts to destroy Voodooism by cutting down sacred trees and destroying the complex apparatus of worship, have given up trying to disentangle one from the other.

We visited one of the *tonnelles* on the outskirts of the city. Our guide was the *Houngan*, its highpriest, a tall, thin, preternaturally intelligent-looking man who spoke only Creole. The peristyle was open-sided and had a palm-leaf roof supported at the centre by a painted and decorated pole. In the surrounding huts were altars, and all the complex apparatus: bottles filled with strange substances, swords, crucifixes, bells, anthropomorphic paintings of gods and goddesses, gourds enclosed in beads and vertebrae, china pots that looked as if they ought to have contained *foie gras* tied up with beads, pincers, iron serpents, old bedsteads with horrible mattresses, and, on the walls, mystical patterns and pictures of the Virgin and the saints who have a place in the ceremonies. In the smallest hut, Le Caye Zombi, there were shackles and whips. And there was, of course, the complete equipment of the Baron Samedi, set out like a gentleman's wardrobe by his valet, complete with bowler hat ready for the day, but mounted on a black cross. It was all very interesting, but it needed the ecstatic participants to give it meaning.

After some days in Port-au-Prince, we set off for Cap-Haïtien, the other city of Haiti, in the Département du Nord. By this time we had seen so many galleries full of primitive paintings that our heads were swimming. Some of them were in marvellous colours, gold and cobalt and splendid reds, and often depicted unnaturally elongated peasants, the women with great baskets of Indian corn on their noddles, standing in front of what was, by a trick of perspective, a diminutive village. And we had listened, fascinated, to the Haitian version of the French language, spoken with the omission of the 'r' sound, something all Creoles affected – 'Twès bien' and 'La Fwance de la Metwopole'.

With a *laisser-passer* signed by the Secretary-General of the Interior, without which it was impossible to travel far in Haiti, and with another addressed to the Préfet of Cap-Haïtien, we set off up the Grande Rue, the road by which we had originally arrived, in the hour before the dawn. Early morning fires were already erupting outside the shanties. On the right was the sugar cane railway which also brought the country people into town on days of obligatory 'rejoicing', as well as on more spontaneous occasions. To the left, now, there were mangrove swamps. Also on the right was the road which led to the Dominican frontier, sixty miles to the east, by way of the Etang Saumâtre which was full of crocodiles. Somewhere here we drove through our first road block without realizing it. We expected a bullet or two in our backs, but presumably the guards were still asleep.

On to Duvalierville, all concrete, one of the Doctor's brain children. Its most important building was a huge cockpit, but there was also an unfinished cinema with pigs rooting at the entrance, a non-functioning restaurant, a church which had iron rods for the reinforced concrete tower, never built, a thatched night-club, still in operation, and a number of houses – more than when Greene was there, researching *The Comedians* – all occupied.

On a stretch of coast beyond Arcahie, cement walls and metal shutters concealed the houses of the rulers. Here, a convoy of black limousines on the return journey came lurching out on to the road in front of us, escorted by jeeps and lorryloads of men with sub-machine guns, and set off for the city at 80 miles an hour – Bébé Doc, Ninth President for Life, on the move.

We arrived at the little town of St Marc on a beautiful bay: sky and sea the colour of pearls. From it fishermen hauled a long net full of fish. The houses were old and made of wood, and there were raised sidewalks under the arcades and an eighteenth-century cannon embedded in the earth in the street. Here we drank beer in a dark, cavernous café, watched by tall, thin young men who were so black that only their eyes and shirts were visible in the darkness.

'Vous êtes blancs,' one of them said, frankly surprised, to which all we could think of to answer was 'Oui'.

A bit further on, at Lafond, there was a market swarming with people and animals on the bank of the Rivière de l'Artibonite. Further up that river was the Hôpital Schweitzer, run by an American doctor, Mellon, who had done much good here in a country where there were only six doctors to every 100,000 persons. Ahead, the road now ran through the great plain of Artibonite, a brilliant green sea of rice paddy, to distant mountains which were a deep blue. By now it had collapsed utterly and we had to zig-zag constantly to avoid huge potholes, one of which contained a fully grown pig.

Occasionally, we passed a village, or a lacou of cailles, which was less than a village, being the huts of a man with several common-law wives, with fires burning outside under rickety thatched lean-tos. Polygamy was common. In such places 85 per cent of Haitians lived out their brief lives (the expectation of life was around forty years).

We reached the mountains and the road improved. It passed through a grim region in which the cailles were few and decayed, and the only vegetation various sorts of cactus, noxious weeds and thorn. How anyone could exist in such a region was a mystery, but some did.

We passed a cemetery in the middle of this wilderness which displayed the grim black cross of Baron Samedi, Lord of the Dead, as did every cemetery in this land. The white plinth was blackened with burnt offerings. In it they were burying the body of a man wrapped in leaves in a small, newly built mausoleum with slits in the sides to hold offerings, a miniature version of Papa Doc's more bourgeois residence in the cemetery at Port-au-Prince. This solid little building was a great contrast to the caille in which this man passed his life. For the majority of Haitians the only solid roof they ever have over their heads is in the city of the dead.

At half past ten we crossed the main ridge of the Chaîne de Belance which separates L'Artibonite from the Département du Nord. The road was paved with huge stone slabs, numbers of which had sunk far below the level of the rest. There, near the pass, it was very cold and the people were very poor. They came running to the roadside at the sound of the engine to implore us to give them money. They did not ask for dollars, as they had in Port-au-Prince, but for a single gourde, the local currency which had an even exchange rate with the dollar of 20 cents to one gourde.

At the foot of the pass we asked an old woman for half a dozen oranges. She asked for half a gourde, but when we took our half dozen oranges she tried to press the whole basketful on us. Surely half a gourde couldn't have been the market price?

By the time we reached Plaisance, a place among thick woods, the road surface had disappeared completely. In some places it was like driving over frozen waves, in others it was nothing more than a river bed filled with enormous stones. In this country it took an hour to cover sixteen miles.

At 1.30 p.m. we arrived at the gates of Cap-Haïtien in a state of extreme fatigue, to find it the antithesis of Port-au-Prince. Certainly the poor were just as poor in their warrens on the outskirts, but the city itself was old-fashioned, quiet and cool, a place in which you could actually stop to think. No wonder that the Cap-Haïtien painters regarded themselves as a separate school, of whom Philomée Obin, father of an enormous family, who worked in a rickety wooden house on the outskirts of the town, was the best known. Long streets of old houses led up from the Atlantic to the foot of a wooded mountain, or else opened up vistas of an eighteenth-century cathedral with silver-painted cupolas, all recorded, one hoped, by some tropical Pissarro.

The ruined palace of Sans Souci, built by the ex-slave Christophe when he proclaimed himself king, as Henri I, in 1811, is at Milot about twelve miles from the city. The road to it runs through the plain of Limonade, a rich countryside in which, until the slaves freed themselves, were the estate houses of French sugar planters. Now scarcely even a ruin remained.

There can be few buildings of European inspiration with such a setting, at the head of a grand staircase and with the green jungle all around as if about to smother it. Even in its greatest splendour, with its European furnishings, it could not have been more memorable than it was when we visited it, an echoing, empty shell.

It housed the despotic black king who had been a waiter in Cap-Haïtien, his gallant queen who never failed him, even in adversity, their son, the Prince Royal, who was even fatter than Bébé Doc, and all the court. A looking-glass world, above the plain of Limonade, with a black king and queen awaiting the arrival of a black Alice.

It took about an hour and a half to climb to Christophe's Citadel, which stands about 2500 feet up on the Pic de Laferrière, through dense growths of mahogany, pomegranates, palms, lianas and bananas. For most of the way the mist was thick. Through it the sound of Auld Lang Syne, played by small boys on the little bamboo pipes they sold to tourists, was borne on the damp air. It was like being on the way to a tropical Balmoral. The track became steeper and steeper and impossibly slippery; but suddenly we were in sunshine, with the citadel floating on clouds above an enormous, sharpened prow of stone which the German engineers who designed it hoped would deflect shot from the curtain walls, here 130 feet high and 12 feet thick at the base.

There is nothing like the citadel in the whole realm of military architecture. No one really knows how many emancipated slaves died dragging the enormous stones and hundreds of cannon up from the valley floor. It took thirteen years to build, and when it was nearly finished one of the powder magazines was struck by lightning, and the king's brother, the Duc de Port-de-Paix, and 159 of the household troops, the only ones trusted to form the garrison, were blown to smithereens.

The king shot himself in 1820 at Sans Souci while the mob roared for his blood outside. His body was brought to the citadel and hidden under a heap of quicklime to prevent it from being torn to pieces. His epitaph, prepared by himself, was 'I shall rise from my ashes'.

Below
Fishermen on the coast of Guadeloupe.
Together with Haiti, which also had French antecedents, food on Martinique and Guadeloupe was far better than anywhere else in the Caribbean that I have ever visited. Stuffed crabs, stewed conch and octopus, *accras* (fritters of shell and soft fish with

vegetables), *court-bouillon* of red fish, curries, roast wild goat, kids with saffron, and all of these more easily available, and much better, in the most humble places than in hotels in which, inevitably, they suffered some kind of change for the worse.

Overleaf

Old houses in Rouseau, Dominica, 1972.

Dominica, so named because Columbus discovered it on a Sunday, is the largest of the Windward Islands, and famous for its very British cricket matches, hot springs, boiling lakes and dense forests. In spite of its olde worlde charm, the capital Rouseau gave shelter to a small but vocal group which threatened to make it an impossible stopping place, to the horror of the local taxi drivers ('Go home, whites!' we were told three times in fifteen minutes), and so, after speaking to the Governor of Dominica who said he couldn't do anything about it, we complied.

Above
Waitress in a fish restaurant, Guadeloupe.

Opposite
Bath time in Martinique.

The island in the background was
commissioned as a man-of-war, *HMS
Diamond Rock*, by the British Admiralty when
a garrison of sailors was put ashore on it
during the Napoleonic wars. They got guns
up to the top of it, using tackle, and held it
against the French for a year and a half,
until 1805. The French, with sturdy
patriotism, still continue to call it *La Roche
Diamante*.

Overleaf
On the beach in Martinique.

At that time the most beautiful beach in
either Martinique or Guadeloupe was at Ste
Anne, east of Point-à-Pitre, but this was
already overlooked by a luxury hotel whose
main building resembled a collapsed *crêpe*.
God only knows what has happened since.

Welcome to 'Foreign Friends', Shanghai.
How were they assembled, these innumerable thousands of Chinese who lined the
roads from the airport to greet not a load of
hardliners but members of the Imperial
Ethiopian royal family, and were still lining
the roads on their way back?

Imperial Outing

China, 1973

IN 1973 I went to China on a flight inaugurating a regular service between Addis Ababa and Shanghai. On board were a number of members of the Ethiopian royal family, various ministers, many of whom are now no more, and the Chinese *chargé d'affaire* to the court of Emperor Haile Selassie.

China was still in a state of profound shock as a result of the massacres which had taken place between 1949 and 1969 during the regime of Mao Tse-tung, when between 32.25 and 61.7 million Chinese were eliminated. The Chairman was still on the throne – three more years were to elapse before he finally passed away and foreign visitors, other than diplomats, were still a rarity.

At four in the morning, Addis Ababa time, on 3 February, I was 40,000 feet or so up in an Ethiopian Airways Boeing 707 over Kunming, in the province of Yunnan in southwest China. During the Long March it had taken the First Front Red Army seven months to reach the longitude of Kunming from its base in Kiangsi. All being well we would be over Kiangsi in two hours. I was glad I was not marching. Since leaving Bombay at 11.30 the previous evening we had flown over Burma, crossed the upper reaches of the Salween and Mekong rivers, and the Wu Liang Shan and the Ai Lao Shan Mountains in China and the Black River without seeing any of them. Fog forced us to put down at Canton, where we found ourselves unseasonably clad for the subtropics, and we eventually arrived at Shanghai some eight hours late on an afternoon of inspissated gloom.

Formed up on the tarmac was a carbon copy of the welcoming party that had been hastily assembled at Canton. Anxious to ingratiate myself with anyone Chinese I decided to get in on the hand-shaking, but by the time I disembarked the committee had dispersed and the Ethiopian royals had been whisked away in a convoy of enormous, priceless (literally, because they were unobtainable through commerce), lace-curtained black limousines, all made in Shanghai. Deprived of our passports with their enormous, priceless (in the same sense) Chinese visas, we journalists and other hangers-on eventually followed them into the city in a convoy of buses, each with a complement of interpreters, some employed by the Chinese International Travel Service, others university lecturers and school teachers, all of whom confessed themselves worried about what their pupils would be up to in their absence.

In the Changning and Chingan districts of the city the afternoon shifts were spilling out of the factories on bicycles and on foot – quiet, orderly, healthy-looking and cheerful, dressed in padded cotton coats and suits obtainable only on coupons. Not a skirt to be seen – nor a dog nor a cat nor the sound of a bird. These countless thousands were held back at the intersections to let us pass, some incurious, others enthusiastic enough to clap. We were told that it was good manners to clap back. Soon it became tiring. There was hardly a car in sight, only lorries filled with goods and people. Finally, we drew up at the side door of the Peace Hotel, formerly the Cathay, the one-time property of Sir Victor Sassoon. Here, the convoy of cars that had conveyed the royal party was being given a sluicing by strangely feudal-looking chauffeurs. Inside, the public rooms were marmoreal caverns lit by 40-watt bulbs, the upstairs corridors lined with brass spittoons. The double bedrooms were clean but sad and behind a curtain in an alcove a couch waited to fulfil some equivocal purpose. The staff smiled endlessly and inscrutably.

By craning out of the window I could see the Whangpoo River, full of junks and sampans and a big ship coming up to a mooring from the Yangtze, twelve miles downstream. The boom of its siren mingled with the hellish screech of motor horns and the tinkle of 10.82 million bicycle bells, not to speak of the Fortnum and Mason-type carillon in the mock Tudor tower of the old customs building.

Just before dusk I managed to give my interpreter the slip and rushed out on to what Europeans used to call the Bund, the waterfront, which was a little like the Thames Embankment outside the Savoy, apart from the rows of men and women, some young, some old and shrivelled like walnuts, all equally zealously performing the slow-motion callisthenics said to be related to the Taoist conception of the unity of opposites known as *tai chi ch'uan.*

The moment I reached the river wall I was hemmed in by hundreds of people. As more and more arrived they began to sway from side to side and surge backwards and forwards in a sort of crazy, rhythmic dance; as they did so, although I smiled at them and tried to appear friendly, they gazed into my eyes without any expression – not a trace of friendliness, malice or even curiosity. Behind them the lights were coming on in the tall buildings that had once housed the Chartered Bank, Jardine Matheson and so on, but were now effectively the tombs of capitalism.

All this left only ten minutes to get ready for a reception and banquet in the Hall of Friendship. Excellent Shanghai food, followed by Chinese speeches and Ethiopian replies on the theme we heard everywhere we went: the Chinese praised the Imperial Government of Ethiopia and its people, under the leadership of His Imperial Majesty, for their glorious tradition of fighting against imperialism. By 10.30 p.m. the city resembled a dimly-lit cemetery.

The government sent an Ilyushin 62 to take us to Peking, as it was then still called. Apart from short-haul prestige flights such as ours, the whole fleet had been grounded long ago because of doubts about its airworthiness and because the Russians had been reluctant to supply spare parts; indeed the vibration in the lavatory was so great that it was impossible to sit on the seat.

The stewardesses were charming – they fed us mandarin oranges (I wondered what they called them now, in Maoist China) – but no promise of anything but their determination to defend their country and help their comrades could be discerned in their almost unnaturally shining eyes and sing-song voices. Over the next few days I would be equally unable to discern any other sentiments in the shining eyes of Little Red Guards in Hanchow dancing 'Little Lin has Put on the Red Scarf' or singing 'I Watch the Geese for the People's Commune'; or of four-year-olds doing down the imperialists with toy rifles and bayonets at the Fong Cheng residential area back in Shanghai.

Opposite
Heart-rending hostess at Shanghai airport.

In the Peking Hotel the service was excellent – boiling water for do-it-yourself tea arrived in a bright blue vacuum flask emblazoned with a picture of a white stallion with streaming mane jumping over a power station. One day two of us borrowed bikes from the Australian ambassador, immured with his staff in a suite of rooms alive with bugging devices, and spent a happy day cycling through Peking. The lights were still burning in the corridors of the hotel when at 6.30 a.m. we crept out to see what was to be seen. The temperature (it was February) was around 20°F and a parched, bitter wind was droning in from

Siberia by way of Mongolia, bringing a dry dust which produced Peking throat. We decided to begin with the railway station because we both liked steam engines, so we pedalled off along the eastern part of Long Peace Street, the seemingly endless avenue that appears to divide Peking into two roughly equal parts.

This avenue, which was about as wide as the Champs-Élysées, was a cyclist's heaven but a motorist's nightmare, as was most of the rest of the city. Cars and lorries and the Chinese version of the Land Rover were confined to the lane nearest the centre, while the other lanes were flooded with two ever-rolling

streams of cyclists, each composed of up to twenty people riding abreast, most of whom at this hour seemed to be men. City workers such as these earned at that time between 60 and 70 *yuan* a month (one *yuan* being then worth about 20p). All of them were more or less identically dressed in hats with ear flaps (the more luxurious were of fur and cost about 17 *yuan*) and long, brightish blue, padded cotton overcoats. Most wore white gauze masks, presumably to guard against Peking throat.

They pedalled swiftly and purposefully out of the now waning night, thousands of them; it could have been hundreds of thousands:

there were estimated to be five million bicycles in Peking, each of which cost, if new, between 120 and 180 *yuan*. As in all communist countries the mystery of how anyone could afford to spend almost three times their monthly income on such an artefact was never satisfactorily resolved. These cyclists rarely spoke to one another. Occasionally they rang their bells. The only other sound, apart from the noise of the trolleybuses, was that of the whirring of the bicycle tyres on the surface of the road.

The station was built in ten months during the Great Leap Forward and was designed by students. We left our machines in a bike park. Other people were given bamboo tokens in exchange for theirs, but ours were British – a Raleigh and a BSA – and this was deemed sufficient identification.

Soon, we were borne aloft into the heart of the station on an escalator, surrounded by a minority group from some distant province dressed in overpowering sheepskins and heavily laden with luggage and infants. Ticketless, we were unable to get on to the platforms at which giant diesel and steam locomotives were limbering up for their journeys: to Moscow via Ulan Bator in about six days, to Canton in 36 hours or Shanghai in about 25. So we left the station and set off at breakneck speed through some *hutung*, small back streets, to find a place from which we could see the trains rumbling past, their steam engines whistling mournfully.

From here it was only a short way to the Observatory, a huge stone platform outside the Old City Wall on which still stood the marvellous bronze instruments and armillary sphere set up by Kublai Khan in the thirteenth century, and entrusted to Jesuit missionaries in the sixteenth.

As the sun rose, the light flooding Long Peace Street, filtered by the dust, was first the sepia of an old photograph and then, as it strengthened, a brilliant ochre.

By then the cyclists had come out of their frozen trance-like state and were talking to one another. Some were pulling little trailers loaded with bottles of milk or wood (one trailer supported a wardrobe with an old lady perched on it) and there were big loaded carts drawn by donkeys or horses.

After a Chinese breakfast back at the hotel, we cycled along the foot of the vermilion south wall of the Imperial City to the Gate of Heavenly Peace, a symbol of the Revolution from which Mao proclaimed the birth of the People's Republic on 1 October 1949; and before which a million people gathered to inaugurate the Cultural Revolution. We also visited the Nationalities Cultural Palace which contained contemporary artefacts from all China, many of them hideous testimonials to human ingenuity. One of the best exhibits was a carved peach stone.

If only we could have spent more time in the Forbidden City among the remains of the Ming and the Ching – 9000 rooms occupying 178 acres, a whole world. Looking at the happy proletarian throng of visitors, it was difficult to believe that in the lifetime of the older people present the Dowager Empress Tzu Hsi had dined on meals of 148 courses, used the monies intended for the rebuilding of the destroyed Chinese fleet to construct a marble boat of debatable taste in the lake of one of the Summer Palaces, and is said to have taken lovers selected in the slums by her eunuchs and conveyed to her in a black, yellow-tasselled carriage, an encounter from which they never returned.

The rest of the day was a blur of

Early morning in winter, Peking. With temperatures around 20°F, and a dry, bitter wind droning in from Siberia and over the Great Wall, early morning is cold in Peking. The wind brought with it dust that produced a condition known as Peking throat, which was one of the reasons (the other presumably was smog) why the inhabitants reached for their smog masks.

people and places: of pedalling through miles of stone-paved *hutung*, in which the one-storey houses had grey walls, grey tiles, and narrow doorways leading into little courtyards, where often a date tree was growing; of visiting the State Store on Wanfuching Street and little shops in which infinitesimal quantities of things were weighed out with incredible slowness, as they were in English village shops before the last war.

People were kind, especially if you didn't try and photograph them without permission. (One day, two soldiers had insisted that we took their trolleybus seats, which made us feel decrepit.) We drank tea with old, erudite men in the antique shops of Liulichang, in what was called the Chinese City, and had our lunch in a very crowded cookshop surrounded by Red Guards, soldiers and workers, all very curious about us but friendly. The whole meal, consisting of *shao ping* (wheat cakes), noodle soup, sausage and a big jug of beer, cost us 34 cents each (about 7p).

Finally, as the sun was shining, we reached Coal Hill, a manmade eminence beyond the frozen moat to the north of the Forbidden City. The last Ming emperor is said to have hanged himself from a juniper tree at the foot of it in 1644. To the south, the yellow roofs of the Forbidden City stretched away; to the north, beyond the Hall of Imperial Longevity, there was a stupendous view of the Towers of the Bell and Drum, the sounding of which regulated the days of imperial civil servants for centuries.

Reunited with our interpreters, we were given precisely one hour to see the Great Wall, and if they had been fit enough they would have made us run. We were taken to the Nankhou Pass, where the wall shot up the mountainside to the east and west, covered with snow and black ice, in a wind so bitter that it caused the photographers' Nikons to malfunction.

From the highest of the towers, of which there are estimated to be 30,000 still standing between its beginning on a gulf of the Yellow Sea and its end in Chinese Turkestan, I wondered how anyone had had the energy and drive to build it. How did they manage it here, thousands of feet up in the Yinshan Range? In this section the wall is 25 feet thick at the base, and between 20 and 30 feet high. Some of the foundation stones are 14 feet long and the facing stones – the interior is rubble – 5 feet long and 1½ feet thick. It stretches a total of 3930 miles. When one of its engineers, Meng Thien, committed suicide by imperial decree in 209 BC, he said: 'In a distance of 10,000 *li* [a unit of length approximately equal to 590 yards] it is impossible that I did not cut through the veins of the earth. That is my crime.'

For the Ming Tombs we were allotted thirty minutes. There are thirteen of them. We descended into the ground by a staircase rather like the emergency staircase in the worst sort of department store, into the Tomb of Wan Li, known, charmingly, to Western ears as Ting Ling. It is, in fact, an underground palace. None of the material used in its construction was found on site: the bricks were baked in Shantung, 300 miles to the south; the marble for the huge, self-locking doors came from Honan, 600 miles away, south of the Yellow River; the timber from Szechwan, 1000 miles away in the extreme west of China. Even the earth for the vast tumulus that covers it came from elsewhere, because locally there was only sand.

Down inside the tomb a notice stated, according to one of the interpreters, that it cost one million gold bars and took six and a half years to build, at the expense of 65 million manpowers, whatever that means,

Opposite
A Chinese carter passing through the Great Wall by Zhang jia kou gate which leads to Inner Mongolia.

Overleaf
The Great Wall beyond the Nankhou Pass where it shoots up the mountainside to the east and west, in some places at an angle of forty-five degrees.

and that the effort involved could have produced enough grain to feed a million people for six years. I never liked it, anyway.

En masse, however, the Tombs were lovely. At that time the rest had not been excavated. They stood at the head of an exquisite valley among groves of trees under the Tian shou shan hills, a site chosen for its supernatural as well as its aesthetic qualities – the hills sheltered the deceased from evil emanations brought from the Mongolian steppes by a wind called the *feng*. No one was allowed to live in the valley and no one could cultivate it. Now it was being farmed by the Thirteen Tombs People's Commune.

As it turned out, a wind of change was already beginning to blow through China. Not long afterwards the expert China-watcher, Claire Hollingshead, reported in the *Daily Telegraph* that two Chinese men accompanied by two Chinese ladies had been carried out of the Ting Ling Tomb by officials, the ladies with their knickers down. Perhaps it was the dread *feng* wind that was responsible.

We were ordered back into our coaches by our interpreters, who controlled us as mothers do their children by a mixture of threats, bribes and palpable deceit. In this instance they told us that if we were good they would take us to meet Premier Chou En-lai, and if we were very good we might each be allowed to ask him a question. And just like a lot of kids we scrambled in and were driven away, cheering.

The meeting took place in the Great Hall of the People, in which 5000 can easily sit down, and possibly 10,000 could squeeze in at a pinch. Totalling only about 200, including interpreters and hangers-on, we looked a bit thin on the ground. We were offered red wine (sweet and nasty), white which was better, although it still gave one an awful headache, and *mao t'ai*, a sort of rice wine (really a strong spirit), and beer. If you weren't careful one of the innumerable waitresses would fill all your glasses at once.

The Premier had very dark eyebrows and looked young for his age – nothing remotely like a walnut and slightly fitter than I had imagined, having heard pessimistic croakings about his condition. After the speeches he walked from table to table, greeting everyone individually, answering gormless, impossible-to-answer questions, and keeping himself going with an occasional glass of what looked like nasty medicine. I didn't know what the hell to ask him but finally settled for, 'Did you really say that you're not interested in the economics of tourism?' I was destined never to ask my question. At the next table was the editor of *Reader's Digest*, hot-foot from Pleasantville.

'Mr Premier,' he said when his turn came, 'when are you going to allow me to confer the benefits of the *Reader's Digest* on the Chinese people?' For a moment I thought that the Premier, who was educated at the Sorbonne, might have some kind of seizure. His mind must have boggled, as mine did, at the thought of something like eight million Chinese reading pieces with titles such as 'Do you need a second car?' His comment, if he made one, was inaudible. At the same time he signified that the proceedings were at an end. Meanwhile another writer slipped out and sent a cable, *'Just had a personal interview with Chou En-lai.'*

After this we all flew back to Addis Ababa.

The great Western Lake in the city of Hang Zhou, otherwise Hanchow on the Fuchun, otherwise Tsientang River, otherwise the Qian Tang Jiang river. Marco Polo considered Hang Zhou to be the world's finest city. It flourished in the twelfth century during the later Sung Dynasty, and, according to Polo, so many pleasures may be found here that one fancies oneself to be in Paradise.

Train No. 2 (No. 1 is the westward-bound train), the Rossiya (Russia) Express, travelling at about its fastest on the Trans-Siberian Railway, *en route* for Vladivostock, beyond the Yablonovyy (Apple Tree) range, six time zones and almost 3900 miles outward bound from Moscow. The Yablonovyy mountains form a watershed. West of them the rivers you see from the train windows end up in the Arctic Ocean. East of them they end up in the Pacific. In the course of the next forty-eight hours, besides stopping at some thirty stations, the Rossiya Express penetrated some of the wildest and least populated country on the entire route.

The Longest Train Ride
Trans-Siberian Railway, 1977

I N 1977 we travelled from Moscow to the Pacific on the Trans-Siberian Railway, under the auspices, although they weren't paying for it, of the Novosti Agency, which was at that time said to be an arm of the KGB. They sent a representative with us, and the idea was that in this way we would see more of Russia and Siberia than we would otherwise have done. Together we drew up a list of previously unseen marvels to which we would be taken at various stop-offs on the way. In the event we saw little more than we would have seen travelling with Intourist.

At that time the Trans-Siberian was the only continuous land route from Western Europe to the Pacific coast of the USSR. Since then, another line – with a couple of gaps in it and still under construction at the beginning of 1989 – has been built from Tayshet, a junction on the Trans-Siberian, 4522 kilometres out from Moscow. Anyone ingenious enough to travel on it will eventually land at Sovetskaya Gavan, a port on the Tatar Strait opposite Sakhalin Island, by way of Komsomolsk on Amur, about 1800 miles from Tayshet.

Its route is across the northern end of Lake Baikal, where there are huge deposits of asbestos, then through the Stanovoy Highlands, across the Vitim, which is three times more powerful than the Ob at Novosibirsk. Here, there is so much copper lying about that a female Soviet scientist thought it was fungus. By the time the line is completed to Komsomolsk, it will have traversed an earthquake zone, seven mountain ranges, and the Lena, no small stream, in what is some of the wildest, most difficult terrain for railway builders in the whole of Asia. One of its principal uses will be to carry oil from the West Siberian pipeline to the Pacific.

Meanwhile the Trans-Siberia trains still continue to make their immense journeys, crossing almost a hundred degrees of longitude and seven time zones, observing Moscow time throughout, which becomes rather confusing. For Soviet citizens it took seven twenty-four-hour days, or, to be more precise, 170 hours and 5 minutes, if the train was on time, arriving at Vladivostock soon after noon on the eighth day.

Foreigners, such as ourselves, to whom Vladivostock was, and still is, forbidden, had to go to Nakhodka, the setting-off port for the ferry to Japan. The distance was 5900 miles and the journey consumed almost eight twenty-four-hour days – 192 hours and 35 minutes. This included a stopover from day 7 to day 8 at Khabarovsk on the Amur, and a change of trains to the Vostok, a luxury train for foreign tourists, for the last 569 miles to Nakhodka, much of the way along the Chinese frontier.

Above
Ballet girls, from the Siberian School of
Choreography at Novosibirsk, waiting at the
station to welcome a band of gypsies on
their way here to take part in a performance
of *Carmen* in the Opera House.

Opposite
Village boys, one of whom has been lent a
bike by the authorities in order to 'improve'
this picture taken in Oymur, a fishing village on the shores of Lake Baikal.

Index

Figures in *italics* refer to captions